The history of C. R. Jacklin & Son at Beacon Hill Farm, Grainthorpe

BY PAT JACKLIN

Completed 2022

WHO'S WHO IN THE BOOK

PHJ - Pat Jacklin

JJ - Judi Jacklin (wife)

CRJ - Charles Randolph Jacklin (father)

TEJ - Timothy Edward Jacklin (son)

NLJ - Nina Louise Jacklin (daughter)

CWJ - Charles William Jacklin (grandfather)

TGJ - George Jacklin (uncle)

WJ - Wilf Jacklin (uncle)

CAP - Aubrey Patrick (uncle)

RL - Ralph Laking (grandad's cousin)

GE - Gordon Evison

DW - Dave Warnes (Birds Eye fieldsman)

Mandy - Mandy Benson later Mandy Gilliatt

AC - Alimentos Congelados (Spanish food processor)

CONTENTS

PREFACE	Introduction	5
ONE	Grainthorpe in 1856 – a Background	6
TWO	Wragholme 'Before I Forget' (1950)	11
THREE	Beacon Hill Farm, a History since 1856	18
FOUR	The Foundation 1911-1940	22
FIVE	Beacon Hill Farm 1938-2008	36
SIX	Building on the Foundation 2008-2020	50
SEVEN	The Birds Eye Years 1977-1990	60
EIGHT	The Spanish Job 1988	64
NINE	Retirement of a Colleague	74
TEN	The GRS Story 1988-2015	76
ELEVEN	About the Author (optional reading)	95
TWELVE	The Future Prospects for C. R. Jacklin & Son & Son	98
POSTSCRIPT	Short update	100
EPILOGUE	Lessons Learnt!	103
ACKNOWLEDGEMENTS		104

C. R. Jacklin & Son's Beacon Hill Farm, Grainthorpe, Lincolnshire, 2005.

Published in 2022 by C. R. Jacklin & Son

Beacon Hill Farm, Wragholme Corner, Louth, Lincolnshire, LN11 7JD United Kingdom

The moral right of the author in this work has been asserted

All rights reserved. No part of this publication may be reproduced, stored in a retrieval system, or transmitted, in any form or by any means, electronic, mechanical, photocopying, recording or otherwise, without the prior permission of the Publisher.

ISBN 978-1-915292-31-5

A catalogue record for this book is available from the British Library

Printed by Biddles, Kings Lynn, Norfolk

Design by Craig Lamb, Kriele Ltd, Horncastle

PREFACE

Introduction to these Marshland Ramblings and the history of C. R. Jacklin & Son at Beacon Hill Farm

The following pages of ramblings tell of one person's understanding of his homeland and heritage. This document was not intended as a literary masterpiece, but more of a record of facts and memories by the author. The sections have been written over a period of time and although in some order, understood probably only by the author himself, there are some areas of overlap and indeed more details that could be added.

From 1086 to 2020 (934 years) the lives of the people living in the marshland area have seen many changes, from salt makers working in the King's salterns to the current trend of people moving into the countryside from urban areas, expecting all the benefits of city living and the benefits of the countryside without the smells, noises and discomforts that go hand in hand with country living.

Consequently, many people resident in the village are only transitioning through for purposes of work and long-term roots are not put down, unlike the days of old when it was common to be born, married and buried in the same village.

This old system did lead to everyone knowing all their neighbours as far as the village boundary and beyond. This fact came to light when I considered writing an update to the chapter 'Wragholme, Before I Forget'. It would have to be called 'Wragholme, Who Lives There'.

Anyway, I hope people involved with the area, the village, Beacon Hill Farm, the Jacklin family and their friends can follow and understand these ramblings, with a few photographs to smooth the path of legibility and understanding.

ASSOCIATED EXPERIENCES

The reader may be forgiven for thinking what has all this got to do with Beacon Hill Farm and C. R. Jacklin & Son? Well, in the course of events, these are places that my trail of life and learning took me to, but all the while the family farm remained the one constant.

For example, Chapter Seven, titled the 'Birds Eye Years', tells of a period of 13 years, when alongside farming, my time was split to help keep the farm a viable option. The chapter titled 'The GRS Story' similarly relates to a 28-year period that saw my time being shared to achieve the same objective of viability.

It is a story that, in 2016, saw me returning to my farming roots at the age of 72.

Pat Jacklin, 2021

St Clements Church, Grainthorpe, circa 1800.

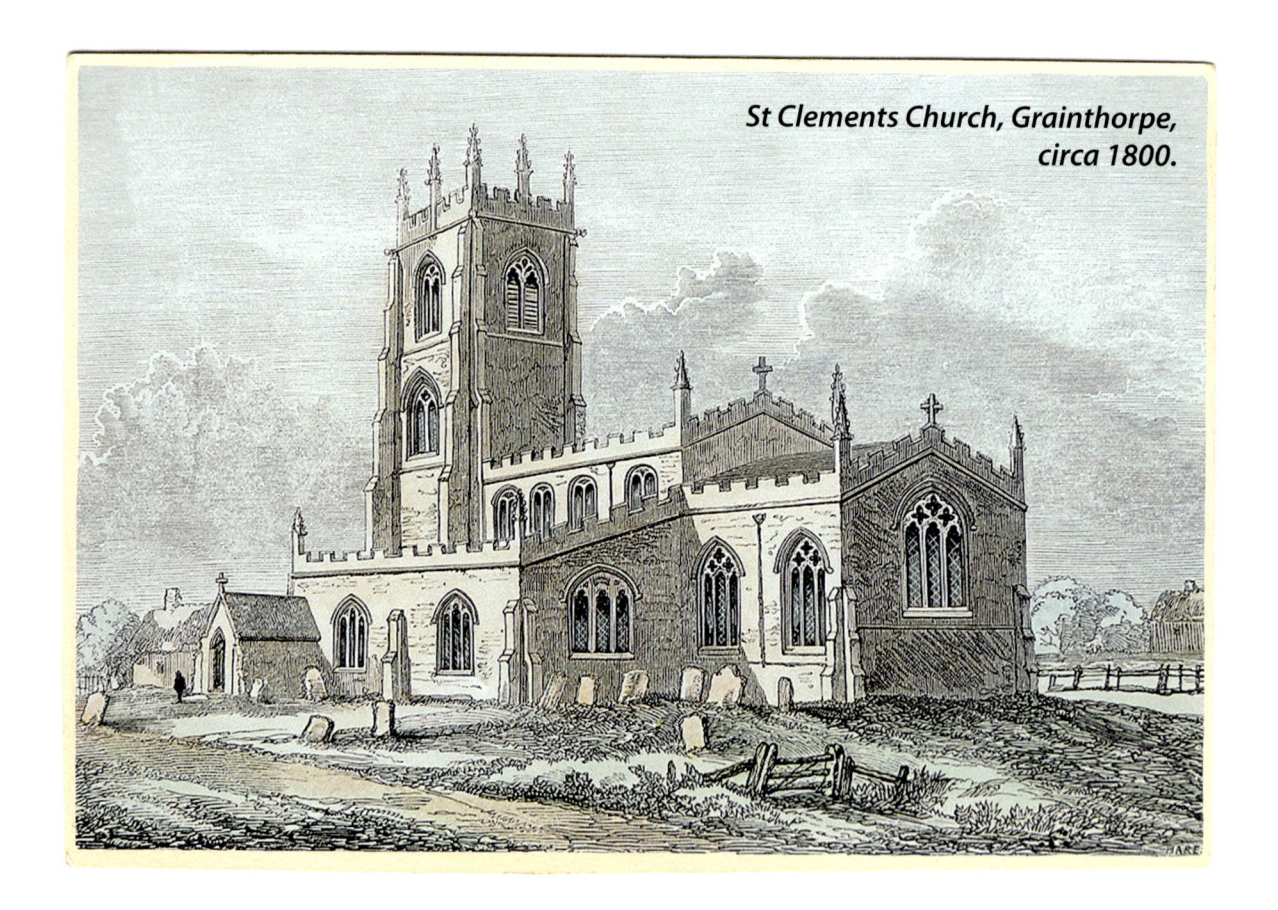

CHAPTER ONE

Grainthorpe in 1856, a background

St. James Church in Louth, our local market town.

Grainthorpe is a large scattered village in a low marshy situation, eight miles north east of Louth and 11 miles south-east of Grimsby. In 1856, Grainthorpe parish had 655 inhabitants and spanned 3974 acres, these totals including 380 acres and 70 people at Ludney and 1024 acres and 98 people at Wragholme.

Much of the parish had formerly been a watery waste called Grainthorpe Fen and Wragholme Ings (note: Ings is a Norse word, probably of Viking origin, meaning water meadows and marshes), but by 1856 this had been drained and cultivated, while the silty creek called Grainthorpe

Firebeacon Bridge navigation warehouse can be seen top right, with the manager's residence in the centre. The manager's house was demolished in around 1960.

Haven had been warped up, except for the channel which crosses the salt marsh to the sea. Plans to warp the seaward side were being assessed in 1856.

Much of the drainage of the Fen and Ings, the marshland and the wetlands was carried out by navvies, who hand-cut dykes and apportioned fields for agriculture in the 1850s.

Grainthorpe Haven outfall towards the sea.

This photograph of Firebeacon Bridge was taken in January 2020 during a very wet winter.

A list of all acreages, owners and occupiers, dated 1879, gives a full history of land that had been newly enclosed and made available for farming. Hence, we see a time when many farms were built or rebuilt to reflect the new prosperity.

Going back even further in time, Grainthorpe had links with Alvingham Priory, with part of the settlement of Grainthorpe becoming a grange of the priory sometime before 1251. Alvingham Priory was established in 1148. Dedicated to St. Mary, it was a Gilbertine Priory and was what was known as a 'double house', having both male and female occupants, who lived in separate monasteries. The Priory was Dissolved by Henry V111 in 1538.

In 1086, Grainthorpe had six salterns belonging to the King (William the Conqueror). It is later recorded that Baldric of Grainthorpe sold saltworks belonging to Alvingham Priory in the late 12th century. The last salt maker in Grainthorpe died in 1608.

In 1770, the Louth Navigation canal was opened for trading from Tetney Lock to Thoresby Bridge, then Firebeacon Bridge, Austen Fen Bridge, Alvingham and then eight locks up to Louth Riverhead or Mallard Ings, as it had previously been known.

From Firebeacon to just beyond Austen Fen marks the Grainthorpe parish boundary on the south-western side.

SOME FIELD NAMES IN USE IN GRAINTHORPE

Temple Holme	*Penny Pastures*	*Gowt Close*	*Strong Pingle*
The Fiddle	*The Intake*	*Grimholme*	*Mary Marsh*
The Wan	*The Onset*	*Bell Pingle*	*Giddy Hill*
Sturkits	*Penny Marsh*	*Ashby Bede*	*Flat Iron*
The Pingle	*Somerhead*	*Rush Close*	
The Butts	*Ming Close*	*Tup Marsh*	

Austen Fen bridge as it was in January 2020.

From the south-west, Firebeacon Bridge and Austen Fen Bridge were the only points of entry via swing bridges to Grainthorpe. More importantly these two sites had navigation warehouses where trade in grain, wool, coal, etc., would have been undertaken. The canal crosses Grainthorpe Fen and the Wragholme Ings, so it was more than convenient that at the end of the canal's working life in 1924, this waterway became a major part in the drainage of this low-lying area.

The canal from Fulstow bridge, looking towards Firebeacon, with Marshchapel and Wragholme Ings on the left of the canal. Covenham reservoir (top right) taken during the flooded winter of 2020.

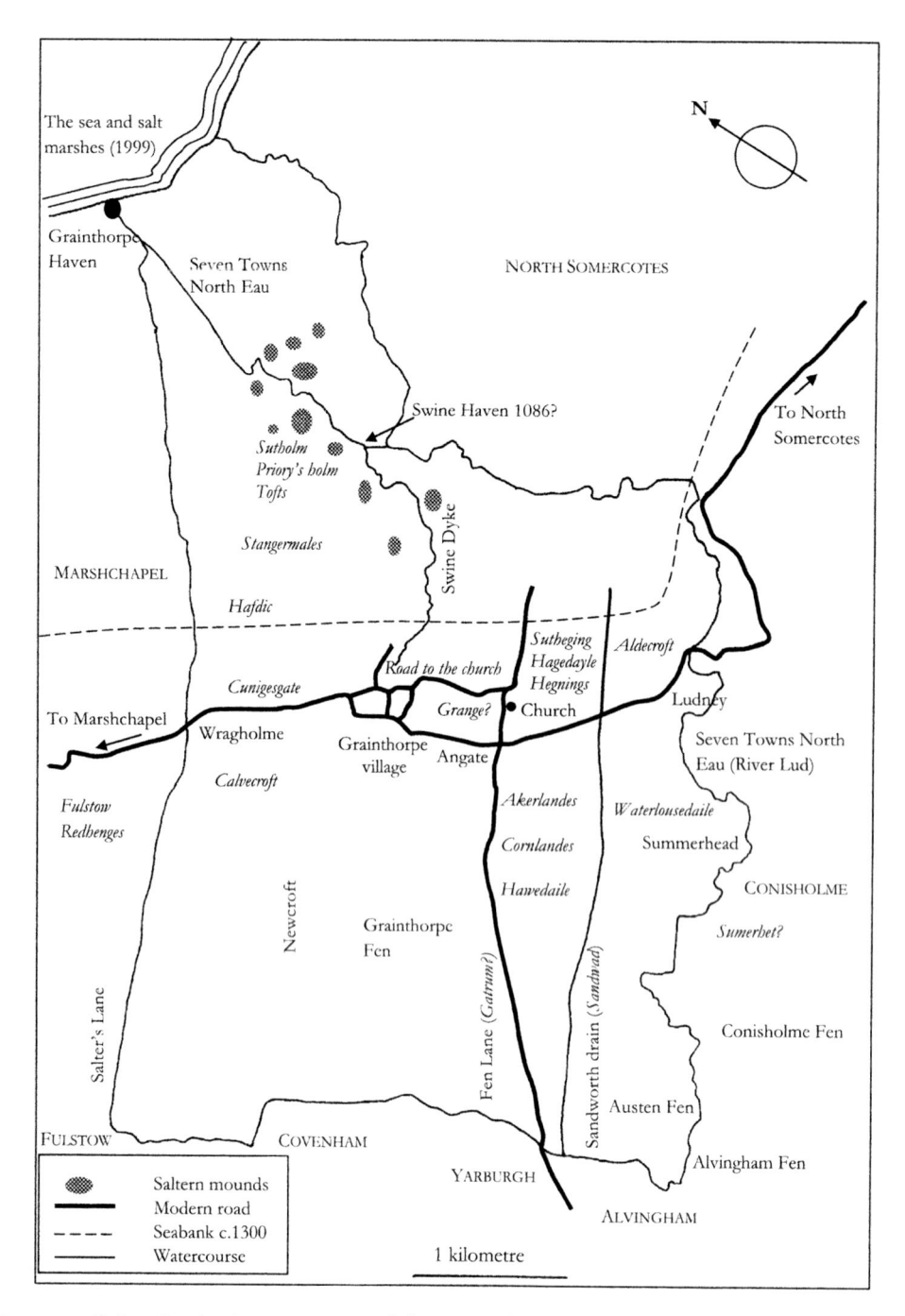

A map of the Grainthorpe area of the Lincolnshire Marshes, circa 1200-1300.
Source: Wikipedia account of Grainthorpe, 2012.

Today, all waterways south-west of the A1031 road have been regraded back towards the canal, where pumps at Fulstow Bridge, Biergate Bridge and Austen Fen draw water into the canal. Also added, which helped to improve this system in the 1960s, was Covenham Reservoir, which draws water from the canal to maintain its levels before excess water goes on to Tetney Lock, where it flows out over a weir to the sea.

Land to the north-east of the A1031 is still graded back to the outfall at Grainthorpe Haven. In the 1990s, pumps were installed at the Haven to allow the pumping of flood water even at high tides. Prior to this flood water could only flow at low water when water pressure allowed the sluice gates to open.

Pat Jacklin, January 2021

CHAPTER TWO

Wragholme, Before I Forget; 1024 acres in the Marsh

Wragholme lies bounded on the north-west by Firebeacon Lane as far as Beacon Hill, and it then follows the north drain to Grainthorpe Haven, a distance of approximately 3½ miles. On its south-eastern boundary it follows Newcroft Lane from the canal to the main road (A1031), then follows the south drain, again culminating at Grainthorpe Haven.

Running from south-east to north-west the A1031 bisects two differing parts of Wragholme (in Elizabethan times this had been the rough line of the sea wall). The land to the north-east, the seaward side, is in the main loamy and free-working soil. The land on the south-west towards the Louth Canal, known as Wragholme Ings, consists of soil of a clay loam, still suitable for growing good crops, but reliant on good drainage.

My first recoverable memories of my 'homeland' is from about 1949, when I started school at Marshchapel C. P. From this date I have tried to recall all the properties, smallholdings and inhabitants in Wragholme at that time, along with any other relevant bits of information that comes to mind at the time of writing.

Wragholme Corner as it was in the 1890s.

WRAGHOLME BEFORE I FORGET

Scrimshaws House on Wragholme Road.

Starting at Firebeacon Bridge we had the Lawrence family's Firebeacon Farm. It was primarily a dairy farm and seemed like a big set up in those days, but probably only had about 20 milking cows. Gordon Lawrence was the farmer and his sister Pauline Lawrence worked as the nurse/dispenser at Dr Gabbès surgery at North Somercotes.

The next properties were a pair of cottages, occupied by Alf Stones and his brother Fred. Later, Alf moved to Willow Tree Farm and Fred had a new house built at the farm by Albert Hudson (the uncle of my wife Judi). Then came Willow Tree Farm, where Alf and Fred ran their 100-acre mixed farm.

Next down the lane was Tom Smith's farm, probably owned by George Osborne and later C. V. Stubbs & Sons. This farm was demolished in 1969/1970. Across the road stood a brick and tile shed and the remains of a crew yard belonging to Mason Osborne, the half-brother to Charlie and George Osborne. Beaconsfield Farm, owned by George Osborne, was on the Marshchapel side of the lane. He farmed 127 acres, again a mix of arable and livestock. He sold the farm to C. V. Stubbs & Sons in 1963.

Across from Beaconsfield was a smallholding that was occupied by Billy Atkinson and owned by the Campion family of Lill House, Grainthorpe. Billy worked for the Campions driving an E27N Fordson Major tractor.

Next down the lane was Herbert and Flo Bocock, who had a mixed farm/smallholding. Herbert and Flo lived at what is now called Gilts Cottage (I think at the time it was called Gosbrook). My father used to work with Herbert, and between them they pooled their few resources to get the harvest in. Herbert was originally from Binbrook, but had lived maybe 'in service' at Gosberton, south of Boston, where he met his wife Flo.

Herbert sounded like a genuine Fen man and could be relied on to add enough to a good story to make it even better. Whilst having dinner one day in harvest time, Flo had produced an excellent spread. Herbert inquired where the new potatoes were from. Flo said, 'You know damn well, you dug them this morning'.

Herbert had a pale complexion and black hair, and it was usual for him to shave once a week on a Saturday night.

I remember in the very early 1950s going with my parents to Cleethorpes one Saturday night for fish and chips on the prom. Who should we meet but Herbert, freshly shaven, and his wife Flo. My Dad said to Herbert, 'Have you been badly mate?' 'No,' said Herbert, 'I've just had a shave.' Flo always found a job for me in Bob a Job week.

Across the road from Gilts Cottage was Charlie Osborne's smallholding. Charlie was George Osborne's brother. Charlie worked as a bricklayers labourer for my uncle George Ireland of North Somercotes and did his farming at nights and on Saturdays. The Osborne family were staunch Methodists and never swore, apart from using well-chosen alternative words such as 'dall it'. Charlie's daughter Sheila was a nurse and later worked at North Somercotes doctor's surgery.

The next property opposite Wragholme Lane, now called Home Farm, was the home of Jack Burgess senior. The farm, a small mixed dairy farm consisting of about 50 acres, was run by Jack Burgess junior. The family had the first grey Fergie tractor I can remember in the area.

All the farms on the North side of Firebeacon Lane are technically in Marshchapel, but when I was a boy it did not seem to matter or make much difference.

Parkers old house in Wragholme Lane, during its demolition in 1969.

WRAGHOLME BEFORE I FORGET 13

Beacon Hill Farm is where my father C. R. Jacklin farmed and where I was born and lived, but more of this later.

Now we discuss the area of Wragholme from the sea at Grainthorpe Haven Outfall, back towards the main road (A1031), again focusing on how it was in 1949/1950. Sea Farm, a fairly large farmyard with two farm cottages, was also known as Fenwicks, who had been the previous owners. It now belongs to S. A. Mossop (Farms). One family who lived there in the 1950s were the Claytons. Mrs Clayton was a Hockney from Marshchapel and her youngest son Graham went to school at Marshchapel at the same time I was there.

Moving up the lane, in the middle of a grass field was Arthur (Art) Peart's Walk House Farm. He was an elderly gent at this time, born I think in 1878. Across a field to the north was Elvidge Brothers' Evergreen Farm. The brothers, Norman and Ray, both worked at Findus agricultural dept and looked after vegetable growing and processing. Their farm was a commercial market garden, growing lettuce leeks spinach and brassicas. My uncle Les Manders looked after the fieldwork and lived at the farm for a number of years.

Move over one more field to the north and there was Sea Bank Farm, which was farmed by Harry Bartholomew and his sons George and Fred. They farmed about 120 acres of mixed farming. This farm had some links with Robert Epton Caudwell, but I do not know the precise details of the connection. Coming back up the track across the horse close was a small uninhabited cottage, the last occupants here being my Dad's sister, auntie Lily, and uncle George Bartholomew (Lily died 1946).

Before the track returns to the metalled road, you take a turn right across to New Farm, technically in

Dauber House, circa 2010, before its refurbishment.

Yew Trees with the new extension that was added in 2010.

Marshchapel, and this was occupied at this time by the Wilson family (of Vamplew & Wilson, the former florists in Louth). Later, Bill Stubbs moved here from Coalshore Lane cottages and worked for Mossops.

Coalshore Lane Cottages were a pair of grey-rendered, sombre-looking cottages belonging to R. E. Caudwell of Grainthorpe House Farm, and standing on one of his fields. I recall Bill Stubbs, whose father had farmed Beacon Hill Farm from 1922 to 1936, living there. Also resident at the time were the Fisher family. Mrs Fisher was the sister of Ron Appleby of ice cream and coaches fame. Slightly later, other residents at the cottages included Chris and Beat Turner with their family of Roy, Sheila and Peter.

Across the road is Dovecote, owned and lived in by Albert and Gladys Borman. It lies 400 yards from the main road, looking up to the Wolds. Bruce Stones has lived here since the mid-1950s. The Borman family were involved in milling grain, building and butchery, all working in Grainthorpe in the early 20th century.

Across the field to the south-east on Ivy Lane (Hiven lane) lies Ivy Lane Farm. This was about 25 acres and was an egg-producing poultry farm, farmed by Charlie Wright. Later, it was sold to Bernard Hutchinson who formed Lincolnshire Turkeys, and today it is a poultry rearing and fattening plant. This is also where my Dad grew up with his two brothers, until he went into service at Wold Newton in 1925 at the age of 14.

In another field across to the south-east (technically in Grainthorpe) stood The Range Farm, with its fine array of red brick buildings. This is the farm where my father CRJ worked as a waggoner when he came back to the marsh after being in service at Wold Newton. He worked here from 1929 to 1938, living-in with the Rushby family.

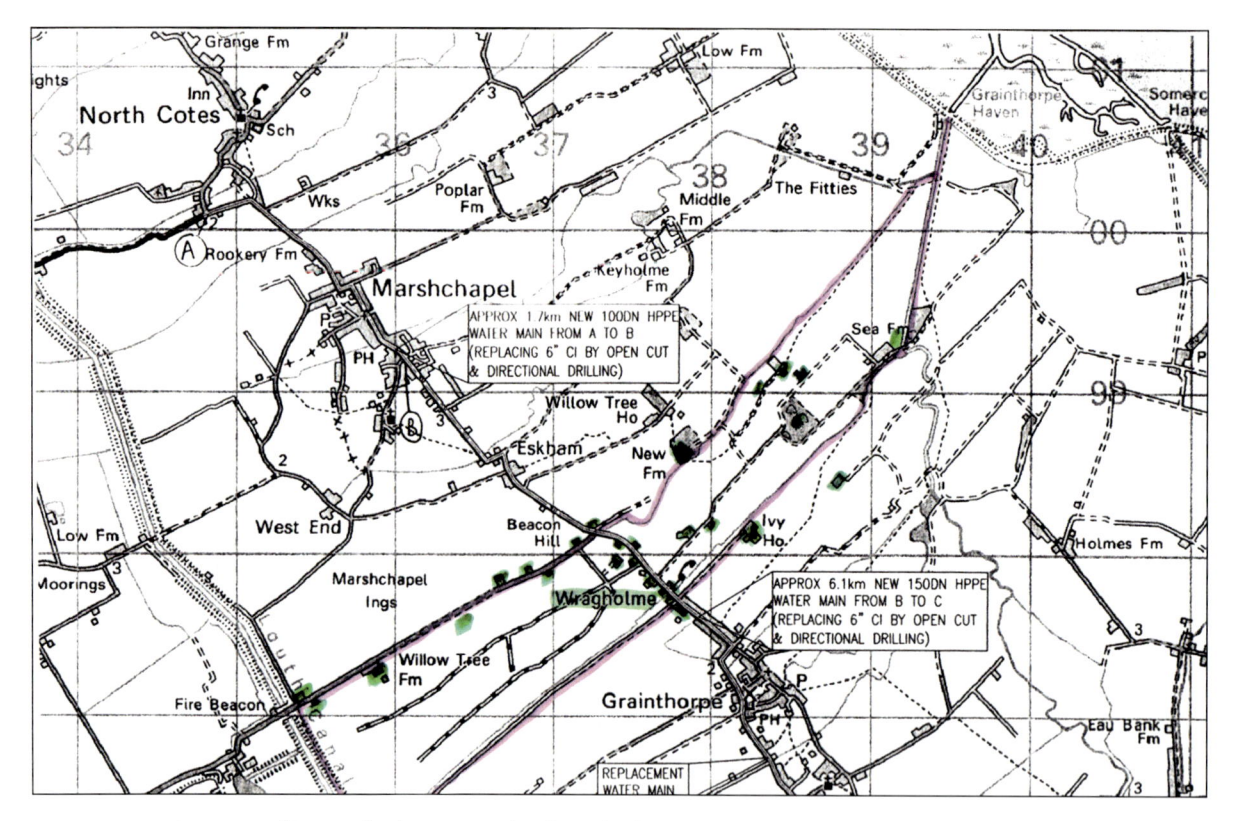

A map of Wragholme, marked with the properties that existed in 1950.

This was also part of R. E. Caudwell's farming estate and although he rented Range Farm at this time from Isaac Sharpley, in 1959 he bought the farm and its 188 acres.

So that is Wragholme from the west and east; now it is time to turn our attention to the main road running from north-west to south-east. The first property is Beacon Hill Farm, Marshchapel, which at the time (1949/1950) consisted of about 30 acres farmed by Charlie Bartholomew and his wife Gertie. They were good friends to my mother and father in their early years.

Next came the 'jewel in the crown', Beacon Hill Farm, Grainthorpe, which my father bought in 1938 to start his own self-employed farming career with 26 acres of land.

Across the paddock was Wragholme House Farm, farmed by the Crowther family – Jack, Jim and sister Triss – who had moved there circa 1929. They farmed about 120 acres and ran a herd of Lincoln Red breeding cattle, as well as growing arable crops.

Back on the main road was Dauber House, originally a pair of cottages belonging to a widow Manning, according to our property deeds. This is now one dwelling lived in by George Holt and Kath Atkinson and her daughter Jean. This cottage is in the corner of the field we now call Beacon Hill. Next door is the old property now called Yew Trees, that was the home of the Clark family – Phil and Winnie and their children, Cliff, Derek, Des and Tony. Then the girls Madge, Ivy and Hazel, who was my playmate at the time.

Across the road was Wragholme Villa, owned by Frank Robinson. Frank was a WW1 veteran and had been decorated by the King of Belgium for saving his life. Frank, a strange chap but all the better for knowing, used

16 C. R. JACKLIN & SON AT BEACON HILL FARM

to come and occassionally help us on the farm. Wragholme Villa, is the house where I have lived since 1967, and is now called Wragholme Corner.

Moving round into Wragholme Lane was Charlie Parker's house, owned by Art Peart. This was a very old house and had probably been thatched in earlier times, but still retained two dormer windows in the roof. The house was demolished by Crowthers in 1969 and the bricks were used to fill a dyke in. I used to buy my bottle of pop for 7d a bottle and 1d back on the bottle from Mrs Parker and sometimes on a Saturday night go and watch their television, which had a 12in screen.

Back on the main road was The Sycamores, then occupied by Albert Cordock Borman and later his son Albert, who moved in from Dovecote, Coal Shore Lane. Frank Kirk lived in the next property, a long low house with a large garden, where Frank grew a great deal of produce. On the opposite side of the road was Brenland, a new bungalow built for Roland Oxborrow and Brenda Willerton when they got married. Everybody, or so it seemed, went to Brenda for piano lessons, although I must confess I was not one of them.

Just across the south drain was a sort of two-part house. The Willerton family lived in one part and the elderly Scrimshaw family lived in the other. I think there was some family link. The old part of the house had an almost open back and in summertime the Scrimshaws more or less lived an open air life. I remember it fascinated me at the time.

George Daniel Scrimshaw died in 1955 aged 84. He was a contemporary of my grandfather, Charles Andrew Patrick, born at Olivers Gap Farm, Theddlethorpe, in 1875. As I understand it they both attended lessons two or three days a week at a house in Theddlethorpe St. Helen. To call it 'going to school' requires a bit of imagination!

This concludes my 1950 tour of Wragholme, 1024 acres in the Marsh.

Pat Jacklin, January 2021

The Range Farm cottages on Wragholme Road, pictured in 2018.

This is how Beacon Hill Farm looked in the early 1970s.

CHAPTER THREE

Beacon Hill Farm, Wragholme, Grainthorpe

(formerly known as Chapman House)

A HISTORY SINCE 1858

The years 1858 and 1859 were when Beacon Hill was built, rebuilt and updated by the owner John Furlong Chapman BA (oxon). It is almost certain there was a property on the site long before this date, as the front wall of the house could well be at least 100 years older.

No documentary proof is to hand, but by the type of bricks and the method of laying it would strongly suggest that this is the case.

The barn and farm outbuildings were built in 1858 by John Chapman, so reads the stone insert on the barn wall brick work. The house, however, was rebuilt in 1859, confirmed by the stone insert in the long brick wall. The house could well have originally been a typical marsh coastal property with two floors at the front and a long sloping roof at the back, maybe going down to one level. This would give some protection from the northerly and easterly winds that can be expected through the winter months this close to the coastline.

The house contained a cellar and had been an ale house in the distant past, probably serving navvies when they were digging dykes to drain the Fen and Ings.

C. R. Jacklin & Son's new farm sign, circa April 2019.

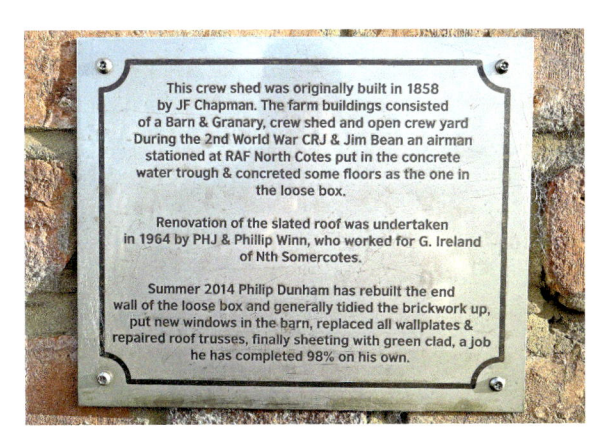

This stainless steel plaque on the crew shed wall at Beacon Hill Farm gives a brief history of the farm buildings. It was installed in 2014.

The stone plinth on the wall at Beacon Hill Farm is inscribed with the initials of the first owner, John Furlong Chapman, who built the house and yard in 1859.

But as has been mentioned earlier in this book, new builds and renovations were fairly common following land enclosures and the drainage of the Ings and Fen, these developments providing a new level of modest wealth that had not been seen before in this marshy location.

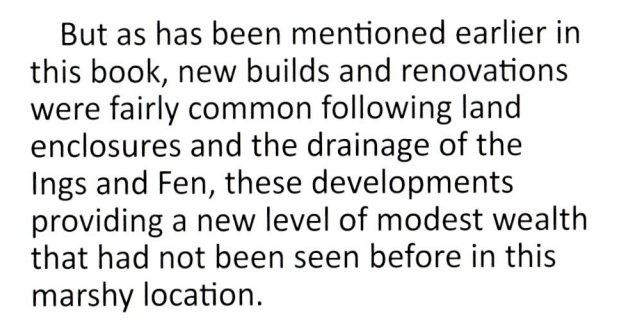

This brief history of Beacon Hill Farm can begin with documented evidence from 1858. The farm was owned, built and renovated by John Furlong Chapman, after which the property was rented to small farmers up until 1922. The early tenants were Thomas Grey (pre-1879), Nathaniel Pridgeon (post-1879), Charles Dyas after 1890 and later still in the early 1920s, George Atkinson. We have a sale notice for the property when it came to auction in September 1901.

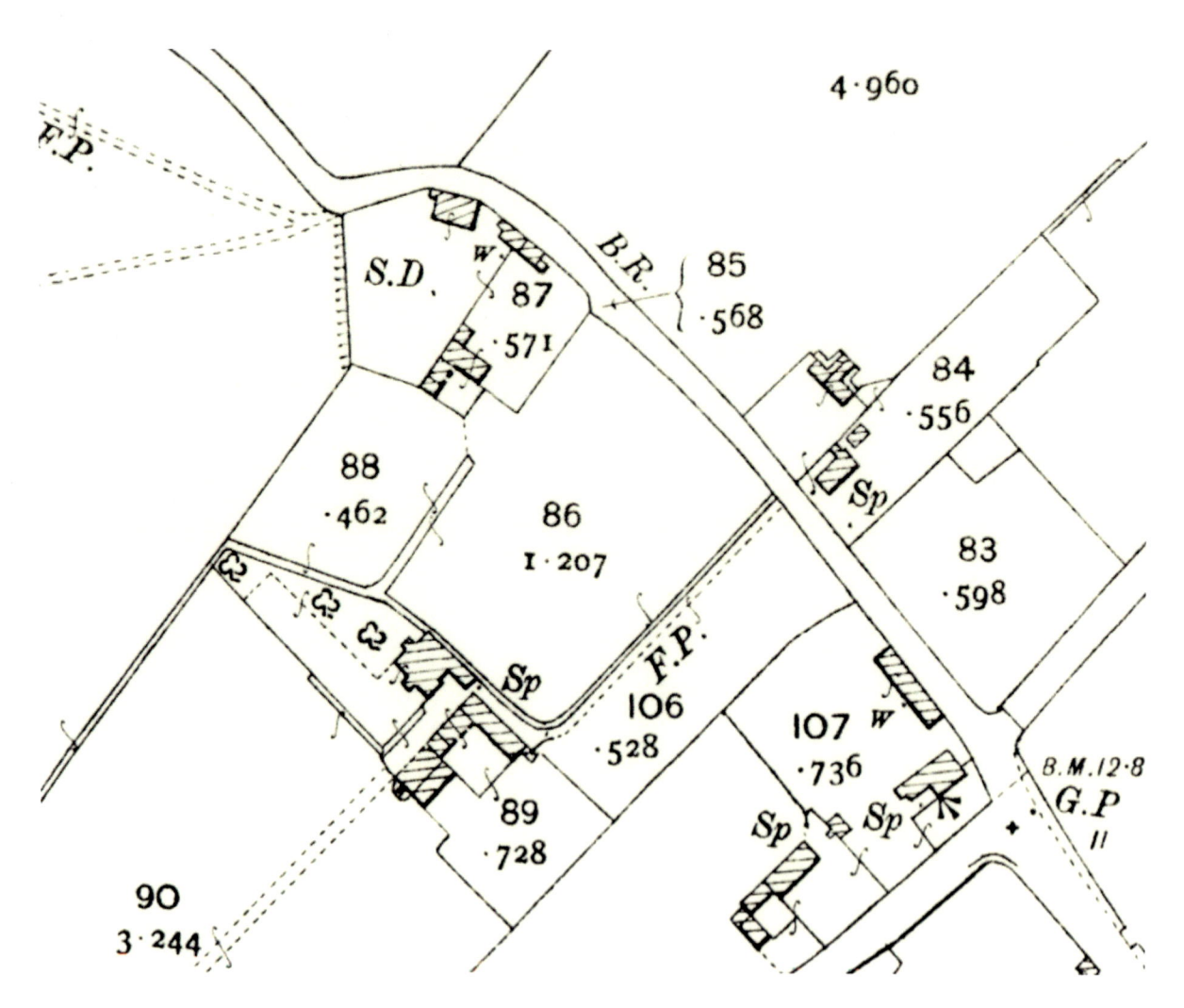

The 1907 OS map of Beacon Hill Farm and Wragholme Corner.

In May 1876, J. F. Chapman sold the property and some land to Thomas Falkner Allison and Rev Henry Falkner Allison, solicitors from Louth, and it stayed in their possession until 1922, when it was sold to the tenant John Dalton Stubbs for £1550, this price being for the house, farmyard and 34 acres of land.

In 1936 the house, farmyard and 26 acres of land were sold to Bertrand Bettinson for £1050. He was the son of the vicar of Wold Newton and by all accounts he was not cut out for a career in farming.

In April 1938, my father, Charles Randolph Jacklin, bought the house, farm and 26 acres of land for £650. This just shows how the depression of the 1930s had brought land prices down.

Eighty-four years later, C. R. Jacklin & Son & Son still farm at Beacon Hill Farm.

The stone plinth on the barn wall at Beacon Hill Farm has the initials of first owner John Furlong Chapman and the Roman numeral date of MDCCCLVIII, which translates to 1858.

20 C. R. JACKLIN & SON AT BEACON HILL FARM

A photograph of Beacon Hill Farm taken in the late 1930s.

A later view of Beacon Hill Farm, this time from the mid-1950s.

CHAPTER FOUR

The Foundation

Charles Randolph Jacklin was born at High Street, Grainthorpe, on 24 September 1911, the second son of Charles William and Florence Jacklin. He was brought up down Ivy Lane, Grainthorpe, with his brothers George and Wilf.

At the age of three, Charlie's father was called up to war, where he served as a sapper in the Royal Engineers, leaving his mother to bring up the family. The boys attended Grainthorpe School in Fen Lane, a good mile-and-a half from home. Some would say that the journey, which was all on foot and in all weathers, was character building in those formative years.

Charlie finished school in 1925 at the age of 14. By this time his father was back home and working as a steam engine driver for the Campion family, who farmed 200-300 acres. At one point Charles William Jacklin was sent to the West Midlands to carry out road construction work using the Campions' steam engine.

Charlie left home at 14 years old with, in his words, a rusty bike, a red handkerchief and five bob in his pocket from his mother. His journey took him to Wold Newton, a small village on the eastern edge of the Lincolnshire Wolds. It was only 10-12 miles from Grainthorpe, which may not seem like very far today, but it would have been a considerable distance at the time. Consequently, home visits were few and far between. Charlie took his few clothes with him in his tin trunk, and the rest was a journey of discovery into the unknown.

The horse stables at North Farm, Wold Newton before demolition, circa 2010. Notice the wide arched doorways to accommodate the shire horses.

From left: Charles Randolph Jacklin (CRJ), Thomas George Jacklin, Granny Jacklin and Wilf Jacklin, circa 1920.

CRJ ploughing with horses at R. E. Caudwell's Range Farm, Grainthorpe.

A photo taken at Scarborough in 1937, one year before CRJ bought Beacon Hill Farm.

He worked for Alfie Addison and lived in with the foreman and his wife, Mr and Mrs Wilson, at The Welfits, North End Farm, Wold Newton. On the first day, Charlie was provided with two horses, the least good of the 'fleet', for in order of precedence he was at the bottom of the heap, below the seedsman and six older waggoners. He set off with his horses as instructed, up the Ravendale road before turning off into a 100-acre field called Thorganby Walk. He was met at the field gate by Alfie Addison, looking every inch the gaffer in his tweeds and leather gaiters.

"Now boy, this is what you do," said Alfie, after dismounting from his hunter. During a lesson that lasted less than half an hour, he showed Charlie how to set the furrow. The other waggoners were already ploughing in the same field. Hence, Charles Randolph Jacklin's farming career had begun.

Some of the fields on the Wolds were huge and a story CRJ once told related to how a waggoner told a new lad to plough right round this particular field. The lad then asked what he should do next. "Go home for tea," replied the older waggoner.

The accommodation provided by the Wilsons was fine. There was one large stone-floored bedroom, four double beds and eight young men sharing the same space. Washing in cold rainwater was the wake-up call each morning, before going out to feed the horses at 5:00am. Then it was in for breakfast and out to work for 6:30am. Later in life Charlie was never keen on rabbits and rhubarb as he said he had eaten enough of them to last him a lifetime while at Wold Newton. His pay for the entire year was £13, with his board and lodge being provided by his employer. This was for working six days a week and feeding the horses on a Sunday, and there was one week's unpaid holiday a year.

By 1929, Charlie, who was now aged 18, was getting a bit more confident about himself, so he asked Alfie Addison if a pay rise might be in order. He got a negative response, so he decided it was time to move to pastures new. His pastures new took him back to the marsh at Grainthorpe, where for the next nine years he worked as a waggoner for Robert Epton Caudwell at the Range Farm. During this time he lived-in with the Rushby family. Charles Rushby was the farm foreman (directories of the time officially described him as the farm bailiff) to R. E. Caudwell. As far as I know these were happy years, even if the work was hard.

Whilst at the Range Farm Charlie specialised in ploughing with his horses (he now had a better pair/team). He also developed a speciality, that of carrying corn on threshing days, from the threshing machine up into the granaries, of which there were several at the Range Farm. At this time wheat was held in 18 stone bags and beans were in 19 stone bags.

Corn stacks in the yard at Beacon Hill Farm in the 1950s.

Corn stacks in the yard after harvest in the 1950s.

Now he was living at The Range Farm, he was less than a mile from his parents' home at Catherine Dale in Poors End, Grainthorpe. This enabled him to make regular visits home to see his family and the new sisters who had arrived since he left home. He also must have found time to travel a bit further afield, such as to Marshchapel, where he met his future wife-to-be, Grace Patrick, from West End House, Marshchapel. They would later marry at St. Marys Church, Marshchapel, on 19 May 1938.

During Charlie's period of living-in with the Rushby family, Mr and Mrs Rushby had a son called Malcolm who unfortunately suffered from severe fits. Charlie was the only person who could ease the stress during these attacks and consequently he became like a family member.

One day, while up in the granary at Range Farm, Charlie was turning barley with a wide shovel to keep it fresh and ready to be used for seed in the spring. He was all alone shovelling and cuffing on his pipe of baccy. Who should appear at the top of the steps but his employer, R. E. Caudwell, who said nothing, but disappeared back down the steps. Not long after Mr Rushby called Charlie down from the granary. He said, "I have just spoken to the Old Man (R. E. Caudwell) who told me you had your pipe on, and that I am to get rid of the 'bally devil' as he will not have his men smoking."

Mr Rushby had to put up a strong defence to make Mr Caudwell change his mind, saying what a good trusted worker Charlie was and apart from that he was the only man on the farm who could carry corn into the granaries. The panic was over, but Charlie had to be a bit more careful in the future.

Ever since going to work for R. E. Caudwell, I suspect Charlie's aim had been to have a farm of his own. At the age of 27 and with marriage imminent, it seemed the right time to make this risky move. The 1930s had been a time of farming depression and farm commodity prices were very low.

Brigg and Louth. 1672/38.

VACANT POSSESSION 6th APRIL, 1938.

GRAINTHORPE,

Near Louth and Grimsby.

To be Sold by Auction, by Messrs.

DICKINSON & DAVY,

At the Greyhound Hotel, in Louth, on
WEDNESDAY, 9th MARCH, 1938,
at 3 o'clock in the afternoon punctually
(Subject to Conditions of Sale to be then produced) the following Valuable

FREEHOLD SMALL FARM,

situate at Grainthorpe, in the County of Lincoln, namely:—

No. on O.S.P. Sheet XL. 7.	Description.	Cultivation.	Quantity a. r. p.
86)	House and Buildings		
87)	Garden and Home		
88)	Close	Grass	2 0 29
131	Close of Land	Arable	10 3 1
166	do.	Arable & Meadow	13 0 15
	Total		26 0 5

If the property is **not sold as a whole** it will then be offered in two lots namely.

LOT 1

comprising the House, Buildings and Close of Grass land containing 2a. 0r. 29p., and

LOT II

comprising the Arable and Meadow lands, containing 23a. 3r. 16p.

The House is a good brick and tiled Farmhouse containing 3 downstair rooms, Cellar and 5 Bedrooms, together with the usual out-offices.

The Buildings include 2-stall horse stable, 3-stall cow stable, pig stye, 2 loose boxes, barn with granary over, chop-house, two-bay waggon shed, crew yard, &c.

The Grass paddock adjoins the homestead.

The Arable and Meadow Closes are situate in Ings Lane.

Completion of the purchase will be on the 6th April next, when vacant possession will be given.

To view, apply to Mr. B. Bettison, at the House, and for further particulars apply to the Auctioneers, Louth, or to us:

ALLISON & HELMER,
Solicitors, Louth.

15th February, 1938.

PRELIMINARY ANNOUNCEMENT.

Paper advertisement for the forthcoming sale of Beacon Hill Farm, dated 13 February 1938.

Invoice from auctioneers Bland & Markham of Louth and Grimsby for the purchase of a mare and some baulk haltrees, April 1938.

Pages from Charles R. Jacklin's note/account book for April 1938. Note the reference to a wedding ring, suit, lodgings, banns of marriage, wine and minerals for a wedding.

A local farm, Beacon Hill Farm at Wragholme, came up for auction, so Charlie made the journey to Louth to see Philip Allison, a Louth Solicitor. Charlie needed about £600 and could only raise part of the purchase price. He had a few savings and was able to borrow £50 from his brother George, for which he paid 5% interest. This led to a stern lecture from his mother who told him he had not been brought up to buy things he could not afford.

Philip Allison shook hands with Charlie and looked down and said, "How can I refuse a man with hands like that." A mortgage was duly arranged for the balance of the purchase.

Although the last occupant of the farm had been Bertrand Bettinson, it was purchased from Bob Hewson, a local farmer and trader from Tetney. The price of £650 included Beacon Hill Farm, the farm house, paddock and 23 acres down Ings Lane at Wragholme.

It was on 6 April 1938 that Charles Randolph Jacklin (CRJ) took possession of Beacon Hill Farm, and he began living there after his marriage to Grace Patrick on 19 May 1938. His farming stock at the time consisted of just a few hand tools and nothing more. So first on his list was a Shire Mare, for which he paid 15½ guineas in April 1938.

THE FOUNDATION 29

This invoice from contractors Hair Brothers of Tealby, dated May 1938, relates to the ploughing and cultivation of three acres for Charles R. Jacklin.

As the world moved closer to war, commodity prices started to improve, but the crops still had to be grown and given time to harvest them before any sales could be made. Charlie's first year must have been a frightening experience, what with having to pay out for seed and other farm expenses, while having no income coming in from the farm until after that year's harvest.

He took action and started working on a casual basis for the local dyke reeve, attached to the drainage boards. This

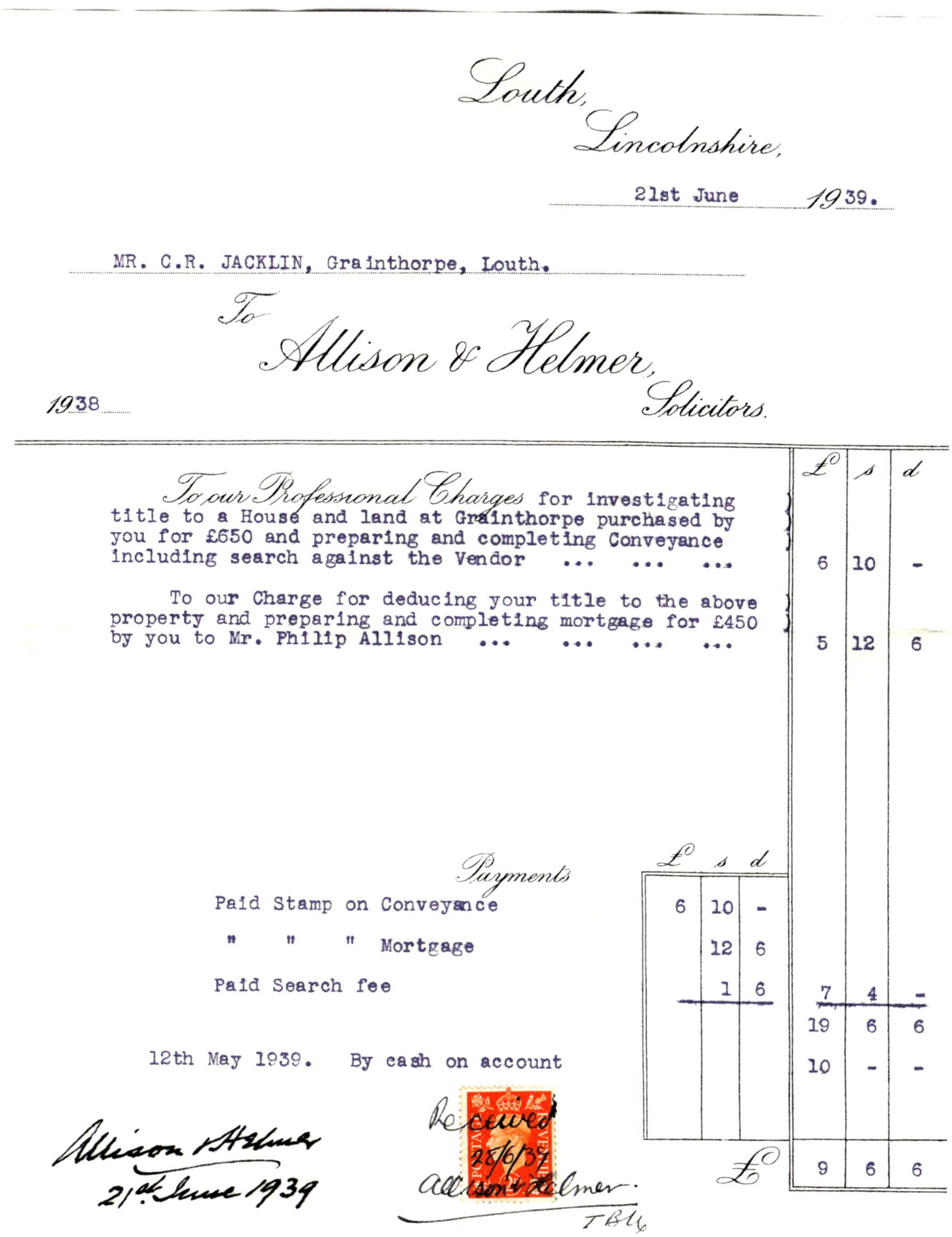

Louth,
Lincolnshire,

21st June 1939.

MR. C.R. JACKLIN, Grainthorpe, Louth.

To Allison & Helmer,
1938.   Solicitors.

	£	s	d
To our Professional Charges for investigating title to a House and land at Grainthorpe purchased by you for £650 and preparing and completing Conveyance including search against the Vendor	6	10	-
To our Charge for deducing your title to the above property and preparing and completing mortgage for £450 by you to Mr. Philip Allison	5	12	6

Payments

	£	s	d		£	s	d
Paid Stamp on Conveyance	6	10	-				
" " " Mortgage		12	6				
Paid Search fee		1	6		7	4	-
					19	6	6
12th May 1939. By cash on account					10	-	-
				£	9	6	6

Allison & Helmer
21st June 1939

The solicitor's final settlement for completing the conveyance of Beacon Hill Farm in June 1938. It came to £19. 6s. 6d.

work entailed mowing the large main dykes that let water flow to the outfall at Grainthorpe Haven. This was how the marshland water escaped to the sea. The banks were generally 12ft to 15ft high so the mowers took breeds with large scythes with blades up to 4ft-long. Standing on one leg, balancing on steep banks and swinging a huge scythe like this must have led to the development of muscles Charlie did not know he had. This work took place through the summer months when water levels were low.

CRJ and his young colt Lion, circa 1940.
Note the small window half way down the staircase to the cellar.

CRJ riding home on Blossom in the late 1950s.

CRJ with Blossom and a load of sheaves, at Beacon Hill Farm in the early 1950s.

In winter, apart from his own farm to look after, CRJ spent many days going round small local farms with the threshing team carrying corn, as this was not a job many people wanted to do or indeed could do. This injection of cash kept CRJ and his new farming business afloat through these early times.

Some years later in about 1940, CRJ was growing five acres of peas, a War AG requirement, as peas are a protein crop and were an essential part of wartime dietary requirements.

The peas were ready to harvest, still a bit green, but beginning to die off. The plan was to mow with a scythe and then windrow the crop, allowing it to dry naturally. Well, five acres with a scythe, on your own, was a big ask, but CRJ was up for the challenge. However, he knew from when he worked for R. E. Caudwell that hung up on the barn wall at Grainthorpe House yard were scythes with a swath board, to enable them to cut and windrow the crop in one operation.

CRJ jumped on his bike and went to Grainthorpe House, the home of Robert Epton Caudwell (REC). Mrs Stothard, the housekeeper, told CRJ she would find Mr Caudwell or 'The Old Man', as he was known, but not to his face!

When Mr Caudwell came out to the yard, CRJ explained what he thought would make his life a bit easier. They walked round to the barn and sure enough hanging on the wall was a row of well-used scythes.

THE FOUNDATION   33

*My mother and father's wedding took place on 19 May 1938
at St Mary's Church, Marshchapel.*

CRJ pointed out the very model he had in mind. "Follow me," said Mr Caudwell, as he stumped off down the yard and into another shed. Once there, he said, "This is what you need, Jacklin."

It was a brand new three-wheel John Deere two-cylinder tractor with a pea cutter attached, just delivered and never used. "Take that, you will have the job done in no time," said Mr Caudwell.

CRJ thanked him kindly, but said he would be more than happy to settle for the scythe in the barn.

I suppose Mr Caudwell's kind gesture must have meant that the smoking incident at the Range Farm a few years earlier, when he had said, "Get rid of the bally devil," had either been forgotten or forgiven.

Pat Jacklin, 26/04/2020

My mother and father at my wedding in July 1967.

CRJ, right, and Paul Carter, my cousin Jenny's husband, at Beacon Hill Farm in 1989.

THE FOUNDATION 35

This aerial view of Beacon Hill Farm dates from 1963.

CHAPTER FIVE

Beacon Hill Farm 1938-2008

On 6 April 1938, my father Charles Randolph Jacklin (CRJ), took over Beacon Hill Farm at the age of 27.

He purchased the freehold from Bob Hewson, a well-known dealer/ trader from Tetney, through Philip Allison a solicitor in Louth at Allison & Helmers. As far as I know he paid £650 for 24 acres of land, the farmyard and paddock and farmhouse.

In those early days he set about farming it with a horse and a selection of hand tools, the scythe being the noticeable harvesting machine. No wonder he often recalled working while 10pm and even 11pm in wartime when double summertime was in place. During his first year he decided to start milking two or three cows, however, this activity presented a problem as the only land adjoining the farmyard at that time was the paddock.

This prompted my Dad to buy the 5-acre field opposite the farmyard, so he had some grass for his cattle and horses. When I say horses, he only had one horse called Bonnie, a brown shire, which worked alongside Beauty and Jock, two horses that belonged to his brother and brother-in-law.

A mid-1970s aerial view of Beacon Hill Farm.

Young cattle grazing in the paddock at Beacon Hill Farm.

Beacon Hill Farm from the air in 1979.

BEACON HILL FARM 37

This wider aerial view of the Wragholme area was taken in 1984.

In May 1944, Bonnie had a foal named Blossom. Then in March 1944 I came along, so as well as the war beginning to take a better turn, 1944 turned into a milestone year.

Blossom bore little of her mother's endearing charms, and she was to say the least a bit fiery and strong-willed. Bonnie, Beauty and Blossom worked side by side until the mid-1950s, when Bonnie died. This did a great deal at my Dad as from the age of 14 he had lived and worked closely with horses, firstly in service at Wold Newton and later at Rushbys at the Range Farm, Grainthorpe. It was a sad loss and it took a long while for my Dad to get over it. Blossom went on working up until 1960, when she was retired. My Dad would not sell her for fear of any sort of mistreatment, so for the next few years she lived the life of a lady, until she finally had to be parted with.

This advert showing IH Farmall Ms ploughing appeared in Farmers Weekly in 1950.

Stooked wheat at Beacon Hill Farm in 1964.

38 C. R. JACKLIN & SON AT BEACON HILL FARM

Stacking bales of seeds hay in 1962.

CRJ and PHJ using our IH B-414 to bind wheat in Robinsons in 1966.

PHJ on our new IH B-250 on the morning of its delivery from Achurch of Louth in October 1958.

The farm's IH B-250 with an IH B-45 baler in 1962.

During the war years, to make financial ends meet, my father worked in the main dykes, mowing reeds and keeping watercourses clear to Grainthorpe Haven. Today, this work is done by tracked machines working for the drainage boards. When winter came there was too much water and this work stopped, however, this was not a time for a holiday. Winter was the time when all the local small farms threshed their corn stacks to get wheat, barley, oats and beans ready to sell or make available for animal feeds.

So this was an even busier time of year, with farming being done in the early morning and evening, with a day's threshing from 7am start to 5pm sandwiched in between. My Dad was a renowned corn carrier, having had much practice at the Range Farm, so he was never short of work. During this period my mother would have up to three service families living in the house (some with children) at any one time. Two families was usually the norm. These personnel were in the RAF and were stationed at RAF North Cotes.

Over the years, long-lasting relationships with these RAF service families, like the Beans from Scarborough, the Fairlams from Newcastle and the Sheppards from Ruskington, plus numerous others, lasted the rest of their lives.

This IH B-450 Farmall in the paddock at Beacon Hill Farm. This was a later nostalgia purchase.

George Jacklin, Aubrey Patrick, CRJ and Charles William Jacklin stacking sheaves in 1956.

BEACON HILL FARM 41

CRJ using the farm's then-new IH B-250 to plough-out potatoes in October 1958.

A brochure for the International B-64 Harvester Thresher. This was our first combine harvester.

During the war, the War AG committees sat in judgement and told farmers what was required of them to feed the nation. These committees were made up of local farmers and a handful of civil servants. It was not uncommon to be told you had to plough up grassland to grow cereals. This happened with the new field my Dad had bought to run his cows and horses. He ploughed the field and tried to locate another grass field nearby. He found a 2½-acre field that the owner, Frank Robinson, was prepared to rent, so this alleviated the situation once again. My Dad later bought this field in 1955.

The man who sat on the War AG committee was our neighbour. He farmed considerably more land, but it was he who passed the news to my Dad that the field was to become arable. The neighbour, although he had more acreage and grassland, never received an order to plough any pasture up of his own – seems funny that!

After the war, in about 1947 my Dad acquired a Standard Fordson model N tractor, registration JV 8535, from Taskers of Tetney. It was about 1937 vintage and had long since passed its first flush of youth. It started badly and when it was cold it was almost impossible to get into gear. My Dad bought a Pierce of Wexford two-furrow plough, a wheeled duckfoot harrow and later an old Nicholson drag. I bet he often thought, 'I wish I could still do this with horses'.

In 1952, my Dad bought a four-acre field across from the yard from the Dennis family, who were butchers in the Grimsby area. This grass field had been permanent pasture and had been used to fatten and finish off beef cattle, as was common in the marsh.

CRJ with the farm's new IH B-414 in 1965. The baler was a B-45 model.

C. R. Jacklin & Son's International 454 using its rear forklift to lift up a bag of seed on a field headland.

BEACON HILL FARM 43

Nina and Tim Jacklin picking spuds in Lowgate, circa 1975.

This gave him a bit more scope for grazing cows if he needed it, however, by the mid-1950s the field was ploughed and put into potato and cereal production.

Through the 1950s, the farming cycle carried on much unchanged with CRJ, his brother, brother-in-law and neighbours combining forces to drill, plant, harvest and thresh. Although the summer dyke mowing had stopped in the 1940s, the work of threshing and corn carrying continued into the 1960s.

In 1956, International Harvester launched the B-250 tractor at the Royal Smithfield Show. This 30hp diesel tractor, or 'The Little Giant' as IH called it in its adverts of the time, was a competitor to the Grey Fergie. All very interesting!

In 1958, my Dad had some war bonds to cash in and he bought our first new McCormick International B-250, registration RBE 5, for £605. We also got an IH B-12 two-furrow mounted plough and an IH toolbar. What a change – still hard up, but very proud!

In 1960, I left school and at the same time we bought five acres down Ings Lane from Campion's sale for £300. The field was waterlogged and renowned for wild oats.

My first two months were spent hand gripping, with my Dad giving instruction on how to trench dig and maintain levels for water to flow. We had nearly finished and started back-filling the grips in the middle of the field, so that most of the field was ready to plough. I think my Dad took pity on me as he suggested that we

44   C. R. JACKLIN & SON AT BEACON HILL FARM

get a single-furrow deep plough on and start ploughing. "You get cracking and Ill finish the grips off," he said to me.

It was cold February weather and there were no cabs in those days. Two corn sacks across the knees fended off the weather. Anyway, the field ploughed well and by April we had it planted with potatoes that we later lifted in August.

Through the 1960s, the main crops grown were winter wheat, winter beans, spring barley and potatoes, with clover and ryegrass grown for stock feed.

My mother always had chickens, consisting of some free range hens in the yard and 300-400 in a deep litter hut. In fact, a new Nissen hut was built to house the deep litter hens. We also kept chickens in the granary.

On the cattle side we no longer had dairy cows, but we did have cows to suckle calves, both their own and fostered. By 1963, we were rearing calves on the bucket, buying locally sourced Angus X, Hereford X and Friesians, as well as some Charolais later on. We reared in the region of 15-20 calves a year, mostly through the winter months, which meant we had around 50 cattle running on 28 acres of grass, with five acres of clover and ryegrass for cutting. We laid down eight acres of ley in Ings Lane and paddock-grazed this to get the best utilisation.

Next to that was six acres of meadow for cutting and then grazing. Ings Lane was also a source of some winter keep. We had the yard paddock of two acres, eight acres of canal bank from Biergate to Firebeacon, and two, two-acre paddocks rented from Grandad Jacklin and W. G. Sowby in the village.

In the late 1960s we rented some land from Uncle Aubrey at Marshchapel. We had worked his land in Lowgate and the South Ings since 1940, so already knew it well.

We grew potatoes up to the mid-1970s when it became almost impossible to get potato pickers. The last year we grew potatoes my Dad and I picked six acres on our own. We decided enough is enough and stopped growing potatoes at Beacon Hill Farm.

Tim Jacklin on the farm's Case-IH 4230 and PHJ on the IH BTD-6 crawler.

In the mid-1970s it became clear that all the hard work and risk that was being put into cattle was reaping little or no rewards, and so by 1977 we did not restock. Over the next 10 years we bought 2-3 store cattle each year to finish in the paddock with supplementary feed, and sold these by the autumn. During this period we had our cattle butchered and sold as fore quarters or hind quarters to customers with freezers who were either friends or acquaintances, helping to maximise profit.

On one occasion, three heifers bought at Louth cattle market were put in the crew shed to settle for a couple of days. When we came to let them onto the grass they went wild: they smashed through fences into Crowthers field where Mossops had about ten cattle grazing, and excited these beast to the point where they all set off through fences and over dykes into another field, where they joined up with some of Trevor Wilkinson's cattle. The entire group again set off and eventually split into two, with half of them heading towards the sea and the other half for the canal.

Thankfully, Mossops' men rounded the sea-bound group up and brought them back, but by this time it was 10pm and well dark. The other group was chased down and brought back a bit nearer home and left for the night.

It was one month before we got our three heifers back in the paddock and subsequently in the crew shed. On the following Friday, they were sent back to Louth cattle market, looking for a new owner. I managed to lose a bit of money on the deal!

During the 1970s we began to grow oilseed rape, a move which my father strongly resisted. The first crop was direct drilled and came up looking excellent, but despite this my Dad

Threshing wheat and batting straw to put on potato clamps, circa 1969. The people are Aubrey Patrick, Charlie Parker, Ralph Laking, Grandad Jacklin, aged 84, and PHJ.

Threshing with a Marshall drum and IH BM Farmall, in picture in the yard at Beacon Hill Farm. Pictured are, from left, Charles W. Jacklin, Ralph Laking, Gordon Evison and Aubrey Patrick.

would not comment or even look at it. I suppose at the age of 70 he had by then seen enough changes for one lifetime. He was probably right.

McCormick International tractors have always been a big part of my farming life, and so here is a brief resumé. Although most of the tractors I/we have owned were workhorses, some have been for nostalgic pleasure. I guess the real star of the show was the B-250. It was like nothing we had experienced before, it had amazing power for a small machine and was able to make use of it when ploughing and cultivating. This was followed by a B-414, which we still own and was treated to a complete overhaul and facelift in 2006. Its original purchase price was £765 – what value for money. The B-414 worked the hardest and longest of any of our tractors and it is now almost 60 years old.

The next tractor on the farm was a 52hp International 454 from the Worldwide series. This tractor, which had so many features that were new for the time, is still going strong, almost 50 years on.

The IH 454 was followed by an IH 585, a Case-IH 885 and a Case-4230XL, all of which have been good and reliable. The 4230XL was followed by our first four-wheel drive, a Case IH JX 1090U! I was going to learn how to plough again!

In 1963, we bought an IH B-64 Harvester Thresher combine with a 6ft-cut, which we used for four years before purchasing an Allis-Chalmers Gleaner Super A combine with a 10ft-cut. The Allis was a good machine, but a bit prone to problems with sealed bearings. To speed things up a bit, we updated to an Allis-Chalmers Gleaner Super C combine, which was a really good machine. Sadly, this machine's life came to an end when I caught a brick wall and bent the bed!

*Four generation of Jacklins.
From left: Charles W, Charles R, Tim and Pat Jacklin,
circa 1975, in the yard at Beacon Hill Farm.*

With the combine bed bent and harvest to get in, myself and Tony Hastings found a BM Volvo that had seen better days, but was still capable of getting the harvest in. Because of the problems of one man cutting and carting grain to the yard, resulting in harvesting time being lost, it was time for another rethink. We decided to talk to Colin Brader, a neighbouring farmer, with regard to him harvesting our crops. This system has worked well over many years.

The best years for farming were in the late 1970s and early 90s. Since the start of the new millennium, the profits from farming have been low and not very 'taxing' in financial terms.

Much of the farm work that was done by Colin Brader and Ian Bradbury from the 1990s onwards until 2006 was done in a timely fashion using up to date equipment. In 2005, the farm became Quality Assured and henceforth another strand of red tape was added.

In the 1970s, in order to supplement the farm income, I did some external work, namely pea cutting for Roy Scaman and Don Brader. This work took place from June to August and involved working 12-hour shifts. We had two pea cutters, both David Brown-powered Armer machines, and used them to cut peas for five Mather & Platt pea viners. We did not have much spare time! I also helped Tony Hastings to carry out pea viner servicing. Tony later bought Fotherby Lawnmower Centre and I spent several winters there servicing grass cutters and small machines.

Beacon Hill Farm, circa 1990s.

*Three generation of Jacklins.
From left: Tim, Charles, and Pat Jacklin in 1986,
with the farm's IH 454 and 585 tractors in the shed.*

In 1977, Birds Eye approached me with a view to running the Pea Control from 6pm to 6am at its Ladysmith Road factory in Grimsby. This I did until 1984, when the Lincolnshire pea operation was moved over to the Hull factory on Hessle Road. Whilst in Hull I became a fieldsman looking after two viner groups, harvesting around 2200 acres of peas. The job involved looking after the crops during the growing season and getting the harvest dates sorted. It was a big responsibility, but very satisfying and enjoyable.

In December 1987, I was invited to GRS Electrical to discuss the possibilities of selling engraved products made on a hand engraver. Well, as you know this is the C. R. Jacklin & Son story, so I will leave GRS for another chapter.

This development and change of career direction did have a huge bearing on the farm and my lifestyle. It necessitated the outsourcing of much farm work, including ploughing, drilling, spraying and combining, leaving me with the maintenance jobs, corn carting and general managing and selling of the crop.

One common strand that runs throughout the period mentioned in this chapter is the need and absolute requirement there has always been for the responsible person to take up the mantle of extra work to keep the farm viable. My father did it, I am still doing it and probably those that follow will have to continue to follow that lead.

During the period 1938 to 2008, there has been many government sponsored schemes, mostly short-term fixes to long-term problems. Perhaps in hindsight farmers should have been consulted and asked how to achieve the objective?

*'Sol et Adversum'
In Sunshine and Adversity
C. R. Jacklin & Son
April 1938-April 2008*

Pat Jacklin taking a break from ploughing in Lowgate in 2018. This was following a black oat crop that had been grown as green manure.

CHAPTER SIX

Building on the Foundation 2008-2020

In April 2008, C. R. Jacklin & Son passed its 70th anniversary, while the completely separate business of GRS Sign Co celebrated 26 years of trading. The two businesses are totally different subjects, yet in another way, their fortunes and paths were inextricably linked.

At the time of writing 'The Foundation' chapter for this book in 2008, we had just purchased our first four-wheel drive tractor, a Case IH JX1090U, and had started ploughing our own land again, plus doing a bit more work on the farm and taking some time off from GRS Sign Co.

In July 2012 I started looking for a buyer for GRS Sign Co. My son Tim had moved on with his own company and our sales and office manager Mandy was looking to make a timely exit, which left the company with a succession problem.

We began by turning to our accountant's specialist department for commercial business sales. Then we tried another company specialising in corporate sales, but both met with little or no success. Finally, we tried a new approach with a person whom I had traded with over the years and I knew was adept at selling. However, it turned out the sales position was not suitable for him or the company. I spoke to three more seemingly suitable sales people, but alas I had neither the courage or belief, or indeed the spare finances, to continue investing in people with unknown sales abilities.

Eventually, a successful sale of the premises of GRS Sign Co was agreed, for the asking price, and this proceeded smoothly and without problems. However, the sale of the actual company itself and its equipment was only partially successful as I believe the value of our manufacturing equipment and client goodwill was worth far more than we achieved for it. This was bearing in mind we had a turnover of up to £750,000pa and were making profits each year of up to £75,000 (the average over seven years was £55,000 per annum).

This gives a background to the eventual closure of GRS Sign Co on 30 October 2015, this event being primarily driven by my wish to get back to farming our small acreage at Beacon Hill Farm. Hopefully, this has given the reader an insight into what occurred, leading up to my decision to change direction and return to my farming roots.

In 2016, I drew up a new set of aims and objectives for our farm to achieve (see 'Running a Small Farm'). I was aged 72 at the time of finalising the sale of GRS Sign Co, so it was important to be looking to the future and how it might unravel, allowing the farm to be successful and sustainable.

Pat Jacklin and son Tim at the celebration held to mark their family partnership at the Kingsway, Cleethorpes, in 2019.

The author's favourite pastime!

The NRH Cambridge rolls putting the finishing touch to the spring barley after drilling in 2021.

Ploughing in Ings Lane with the Lemken Europal 7.

The Cousins type 28 Packa Rolla working in Ings Lane, 2019.

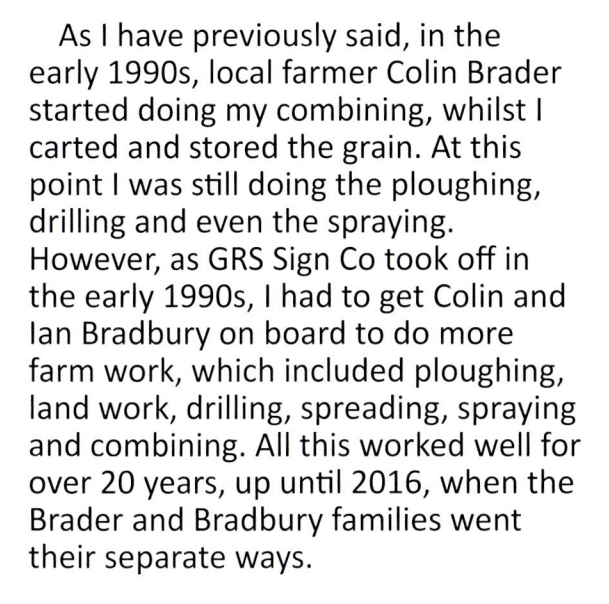

Drilling is carried out using this 3m Amazone D7 mounted seed drill.

As I have previously said, in the early 1990s, local farmer Colin Brader started doing my combining, whilst I carted and stored the grain. At this point I was still doing the ploughing, drilling and even the spraying. However, as GRS Sign Co took off in the early 1990s, I had to get Colin and Ian Bradbury on board to do more farm work, which included ploughing, land work, drilling, spreading, spraying and combining. All this worked well for over 20 years, up until 2016, when the Brader and Bradbury families went their separate ways.

Through the 1990s and the 2000s the farm equipment we had previously used at Beacon Hill Farm had become obsolete or had been sold off, but due to us using a contractor this had not been a problem. In 2010, I bought a second-hand, but as-new, Lemken plough. Without realising it myself at the time, I intended to get back into harness doing some farm work again. Later, in 2014, I bought a set of NRH hydraulic folding Cambridge rolls – gone were the days of gang rolls and pulling the pup rolls by hand, and then doing your back in whilst connecting them up to the tractor.

In 2012, we part-exchanged our Case IH 1090u for a Case IH JXU95 from Farmstar at Brigg. From 2014, I made several machinery investments and this continued up until 2020. Machinery purchased during this time included the following items: Cousins Packa Rolla Type 28 (3.4m), MF 520 Disc Harrows (3.9m), a Maschio power harrow (3m), a Maschio flail mower (2.1m), a Browns Viceroy two-leg subsoiler, a Browns Consort single-leg mole plough, an Amazone D7 3000 drill (3m), and an Amazone ZAM 1500 fertiliser spreader.

Apart from spraying, which is now done by farmer and contractor Roy Scaman, and combining, carting, drying and grain storage, which is done by Conisholme Farms, we are once again in charge of our own destiny at Beacon Hill Farm.

Conisholme Farms' Massey Ferguson Ideal 9 combine harvester with its 40ft header and almost 10t grain tank working during the 2020 harvest.

In 2016, we replaced our Case IH JXU95 with an updated Case IH Farmall 105U Pro from local dealer Louth Tractors.

My interest over the years in all things International Harvester has been somewhat of an obsession. The company's equipment and its adverts first caught my eye while reading Farmers Weekly in the 1950s, and my interest was further fuelled in 1958,

OVER THE YEARS WE'VE HAVE HAD, AND IN SOME CASES CONTINUE TO OWN, THE FOLLOWING INTERNATIONAL HARVESTER AND CASE-IH TRACTORS:

YEAR	MODEL	POWER	NOTES
1965	IH B-414	40hp	Still on the farm
1974	IH 444	40hp	
1976	IH 454	52hp	Still on the farm
1983	IH 585	60hp	
1987	Case-IH 885	82hp	
1994	Case-IH 4230XL	82hp	
2008	Case IH JX1090u	90hp	
2012	Case IH JXU95	95hp	
2016	Case IH 105U Pro	105hp	
2020	Case IH 856XL Plus	85hp	Bought second-hand

OVER THE YEARS A FEW NOSTALGIA MACHINES, ALL BOUGHT SECOND-HAND, HAVE PASSED THROUGH BEACON HILL FARM, THESE BEING:

1955	IH Farmall M	36hp	Sold in 2018
1967	IH BTD-6 crawler	50hp	Sold in 2020
1962	IH Farmall B-450	50hp	Sold in 2020

Our Case-IH 4230XL at Wragholme Corner, circa 1998.

Case IH JX 1090U in Lowgate, circa 2008.

when my Dad bought our first new International B-250, all of 30hp.

In November 2020, we made a decision to sell the BTD-6 crawler and the IH Farmall B-450 and we used the proceeds raised (£8000) to put towards a second-hand working tractor for Tim. The replacement, a Case-IH 856XL, came from Oakfields of Nuthampstead in Hertfordshire, and although it is 25 years old, it is in good, clean and straight condition.

In 2016, we got Braders Drainage to put in some grips (tile drains) in the bottom of our South Ings field. They installed four laterals and an outfall. In 2018, we installed a further eight laterals and another outfall. Drainage is costly, but necessary to grow good crops.

Another new idea from my aims and objectives list was to improve the quality of our soil. So, in 2016 we embarked on a three-year programme of growing 20 acres of Black Oats as a break crop. These were to be cut up to three times and used for green manure. The crop would then be disc harrowed in, sub-soiled, then ploughed. The other reason for this move was to help in combating blackgrass, as it meant we could achieve a nil return of blackgrass seed to the soil.

This Browns single-leg mole plough with expander is used to break through compacted layers, improving the drainage.

The Case IH JXU 95 in the yard at Beacon Hill Farm in 2014.

BUILDING ON THE FOUNDATION 55

RUNNING A SMALL FARMING BUSINESS

1 PLANNING
Cropping: Growing crops that suit the land, are readily marketed and fit with good farming practice.

Purchasing: Fertiliser, seed, chemical, fuel, all to be timely on the farm and ready before needed. To use best buying time to get best prices.

Selling: Be sure markets and movements are available for crops selected. Carefully select suitable merchant or merchants that can handle sales and honour timely payments.

Notes: File VAT return every 3 months (try and make this work in your favour).

2 AGREEMENTS
Have agreements or arrangements in place, well before they are needed. (whether formal or informal)

Typical farming agreements:
- Contractor for drilling, spraying, combining, etc.
- Agronomist
- Grain handling and drying
- Insurance
- Drainage (LMDB)
- Electricity supply

3 RECORDING
Record farm performance
(to include crop records)
Keep a weekly or monthly cash book
(this will be needed for year end accounts)
VAT book for quarterly return
RPA forms and recording
DEFRA annual census
NSF records for annual quality audit

Notes: Make records work for the benefit of the farm and ultimately use them to identify profitable operations.

4 CULTIVATIONS AND HARVESTING
Ploughing
Cultivate
(disc harrow, press roll, roll, power harrow, etc.)
Drill, spray, combine, cart, etc.

5 MAINTENANCE
Dykes
Lanes
Hedges
Boundaries
Buildings

6 MACHINERY MAINTENANCE
Tractors
Plough
Cultivation equipment
Barn equipment

7 SUPPLIERS
Louth Tractors
Peacock & Binnington
Lincolnshire Motors
Tate Fuel Oils
Opus Electricity
NSF Quality Audit (Red Tractor)
Conisholme Farms (contract)
Eaubridge farm (contract)
SP Chapman and Sons (contract)
Agrii (agronomy)

Notes: Suppliers are most important and good relationships are essential.

This list is intended to assist and is not set in stone, and it is also not exhaustive.

Pat Jacklin, 2021

One of our latest second-hand purchases, a Case-IH 856XL, power harrowing in spring 2021.

Consequently, we went four years with no autumn drilled crops, which further helped to prevent the germination of blackgrass seed. As luck would have it, growing spring barley again after 40 years turned out to be a good move because although the gross income is lower, the inputs are also much reduced. Over the past three years we have achieved an average yield of 3.1t/acre.

When our contracting arrangement with Colin Brader came to an end, Phil Davey from Eaubridge Farm did a great job of drilling, spreading and handling and storing fertiliser for us for three years. We have now been able to relieve him of his duties, although he does still handle and store our fertiliser. Also, as a result of needing someone else to harvest our crops, Conisholme Farms agreed to do our combining. It was a bit of a shock to the system when, in 2017, they turned up with a modern Case IH combine with a 41ft header! They also cart, handle, store and dry our grain.

In November 2016, our long-time friend and agronomist Fred Cooper passed away, this being a very sad loss, not least because of the long and successful working relationship we had enjoyed with him, and our trust in his ability.

The Case IH 105U pro drilling Explorer spring barley in 2021.

BUILDING ON THE FOUNDATION

C. R. Jacklin & Son's Case-IH 856XL and 105U Pro in the yard at Beacon Hill Farm, 2021.

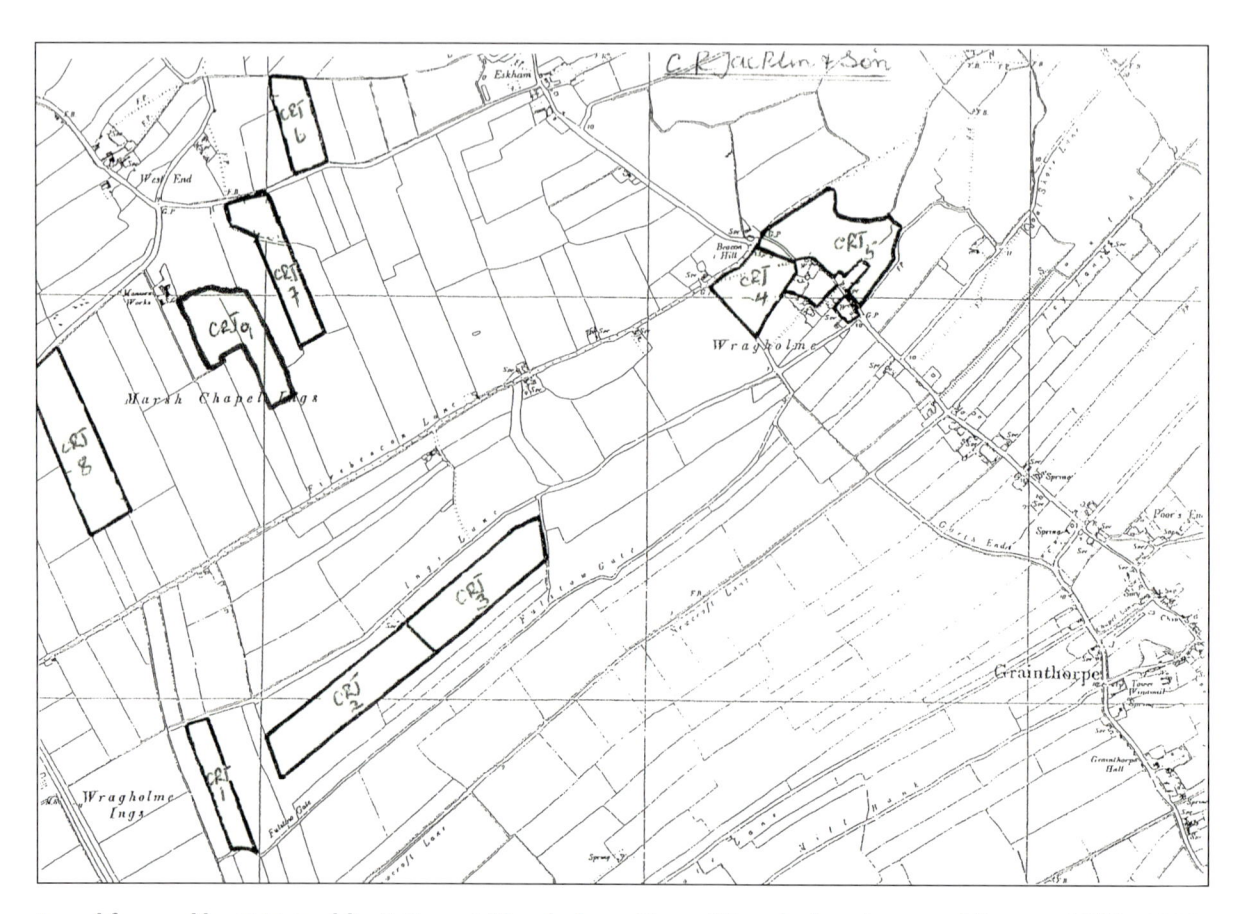

Land farmed by C. R. Jacklin & Son at Marshchapel Ings, Wragholme Ings and Beacon Hill in 2022.

Fred had by this time introduced us to his understudy Charles Roe, a very pleasant young man who looked after us for two years before he moved back to his family farm. But, as they say, every cloud has a silver lining and I think we found ours with our new agronomist.

Stuart McDowall, who is in his late twenties and full of enthusiasm and knowledge, has been a really positive influence on our recent farming decisions.

The need for ever more suitable break crops led us to offer acreages for growing vining peas to Caudwell Produce for 2019 and 2020. It cannot be stressed enough the benefits that vining peas bring to the following crops in the rotation. We have been fortunate that the pea harvest in both of the aforementioned years took place in dry conditions and consequently there was no damage to the soil structure.

Another change that occurred in 2018 was the retirement of Steve Czornyj, our accountant and friend of many years. The trust that is built up over many years of working with the same person can be hard to follow, and even harder for people of my age. However, up to now, all is running smoothly.

The biggest and most important happening in recent years came on Saturday 8 September 2018, when my son Tim and his wife Lisa came to discuss the plans for the future of the farm. This meeting was long overdue and what a relief. Our discussions covered my hopes and desires for the future of C. R. Jacklin & Son, and Tim's aspirations for his input, alongside his existing business commitments.

Moving forward we organised a breakfast meeting at The Mill in Grainthorpe, followed by a discussion group at Wragholme Corner. Those present were Steve Czornyj (accountant), Stuart McDowall (agronomist), Phil Davey (friend and contractor), Judi, Lisa, Tim and myself. We had a list of topics to discuss and ideas and advice were batted about for Tim and I to take on board. Tim's first input was to pursue the rental of the Church Field (10.25 acres) at Lowgate in Marshchapel. This he successfully did and we now farm this field.

In January 2019, we organised a partnership agreement which went live on 6 April 2019. On Sunday 7 April, Tim and Lisa took Judi and myself to lunch at the Kingsway at Cleethorpes, to celebrate the future of C. R. Jacklin & Son & Son.

An aerial view of Beacon Hill Farm and Wragholme Corner.
Source: Google Maps 2019.

BUILDING ON THE FOUNDATION 59

CHAPTER SEVEN

The Birds Eye Years 1977-1990

It was a Thursday night after a club sailing session at Covenham Reservoir. As so often happened, about a dozen or so dinghy sailors would retire to the Plough Inn at Covenham for a glass of amber nectar to discuss the evenings successes and disasters. On one such night, my nautical friends, George Winter and Dick Ward, sidled-up to me with an unnerving smile on their faces. Initially, the conversation was about sailing, in particular the Minisail/Minisprint single-handed dinghy that both George and I sailed. The talk moved on to peas, not the dried or mushy type, but the frozen ones.

George and Dick both worked for the agricultural department of Birds Eye at its Ladysmith Road factory in Grimsby. They both knew I was involved in farming, but also that I worked with pea cutters and pea viners.

"We think we have a job that would suit you," Dick opened up, before they went on to explain the job they had in mind.

The job was to look after the pea control for the agricultural department from 6pm to 6am throughout the harvest period, which would last for about six weeks each year. I decided I would need time to think about the possibility as I was destined to start as an assistant fitter/mechanic for Binbrook Pea Growers, working alongside Tony Hastings.

After a few days I contacted George and said I would be interested if he could give me a few more details. A meeting was set up with Ken Gauld, the agricultural department manager at Grimsby. The meeting duly went well and I was offered the post for

FMC long drum pea viners at sunset.

the forthcoming season. I would be working on a self-employed basis as a member of the agricultural team at Grimsby.

I initially went in at the start of the pea season when only a few groups had started harvesting, receiving guidance from Ken Gauld and Dick Ward, and meeting fieldsmen and production staff. I well remember feeling like a spare part at a wedding, with phones ringing, radios buzzing and the constantly-changing harvest board keeping a track on group movements and results. After a couple of days I must have been getting the hang of it as Ken Gauld said, "Right, tomorrow night 6pm, I think you are ready."

The shift started at 6pm with a briefing from Ken, who filled in the details on the harvest board and all the possibilities that might occur in the next 12-16 hours.

It was then up to me to update the harvest board as information came in, and update the next two or three field moves for each group. In the hours between 8pm and 10pm each fieldsman would radio in to get his group's latest results and update on any anomalies that could happen before morning.

The hours between 10pm and 4am could drag as by this time your body fancied a nap. This could not happen as information still had to be updated regularly and immediate challenges dealt with. Such challenges included low tenderometer reading (TR), a high TR, high rough waste figures and how to cure such problems.

From 4:30am, all information had to be updated and accurate, ready for the rush of calls from fieldsmen which started from around 5:30am. This

Peas being carried along a water flume.

frenzied time would start with a usual set pattern of fieldsmen calling in, always starting with Bill Blow, who was followed by a string of others up to 6:30am.

Behind the field office was the production control manned by students earning a bit of extra cash. It was their job to maintain the links from the field department to production, so that they knew what tonnages to expect and at what time.

When I started my shift I had a briefing from Ken Gauld, who I always took over from, and he would put me in the picture of the plan for the next 12 hours across all 10 viner groups. Our priority was to achieve high targets of Birds Eye 'F' grade peas, which were the ones that made it into a Birds Eye pack. As the season progressed, the changes in the variety of peas were also discussed, particularly as these would lead to changes in the TR requirements, usually as a result of tasting panel tests carried out the previous day. It wasn't always easy to understand Ken's underlying thoughts, but he was always very helpful and always there to support his staff.

A Ploeger pea viner.

From my perspective, coming from a small family farming background and having a basic understanding of agriculture following my earlier completion of City & Guilds courses in Crop Husbandry, Animal Husbandry, Farm Machinery and Farm Records & Accounts at Riseholme, not to mention hands-on work on our family farm, I was able to translate my instructions as I saw fit to benefit the company and to Ken Gauld's satisfaction.

At the time I joined Birds Eye we had 10 viner groups harvesting peas from Louth in the south to Barton-upon-Humber in the north and to Gainsborough and Scunthorpe in the west. The system usually consisted of two pea cutters and two, three or four tractor-pulled viners. The viners were mostly FMCs, although the Lilac group, which was a Birds Eye group, used Mather & Platt machines. Within a few years all the groups had upgraded to self-propelled harvesters with higher capacities.

The next update was in the use of picker heads which instead of cutting the crop used fingers to pull the pods from the straw onto a conveyor into the drum. This method obviously resulted in less material entering the machine so it presented another opportunity to upgrade the capacity.

The picker heads did present some challenges. On Wold land especially, many small stones arrived with the peas due to the pickers flicking the stones as they harvested the peas. However, Birds Eye's engineering dept got to work and very successfully developed stone traps to go in the water flumes that carried the peas through the washing and blanching process and up to the point of freezing. The above modernisation process did, however, lead to a reduction in harvesting groups, with far more peas being harvested by fewer machines, a trend that continues to the present day.

In 1985, the pea operation at Grimsby was closed down and relocated to Hessle Road in Hull. As well as the factory jobs at Grimsby being on the line, the growers and field staff were also concerned about their futures.

As it turned out, probably 60% of the pea growers were offered contracts to supply into the Hull factory. The field staff, as I recall, were pretty much accommodated at Hull. This included Bill Blow, Brian Wheatley and Pete Brown, with only Tom Taylor deciding to leave Birds Eye in order to join Wold Farm Foods.

Tom Taylor contacted me to see if I would be interested in a job at Wold Farm Foods, and an interview with that company's agricultural manager was arranged. Unfortunately, the job was of no interest to me.

At this stage, it was looking like early retirement for PHJ! The next day I got a call from Ken Gauld asking if I would meet him at Ladysmith Road to discuss transferring to Hull. Ken and I went to Hull to meet Colin Wright, the agricultural manager there. It was agreed that I would continue the field control position at the Hull factory. This job never actually started as I was then asked if I would like to look after the Blue Group, from post-drilling through to harvest.

The Blue Group chairman was Peter Clappison, who was also chairman of the pea grower's. It was very well run and managed. I thought how lucky I was to have such a group, but I also knew that if I made any mistakes, the grower's chairman was very close to my agricultural manager!

Dave Warnes eased me in with details of crops and growers and all in all it was a smooth transition for me. I will not venture to say if it was as sweet for Birds Eye and the growers, but I certainly hope it was.

Added to all this came another bonus I was asked to look after the White Group for the first two or three weeks while they vined their way north from Caenby Corner to South Ferriby on the Humber Bank, before going back to join Dave Warnes in Holderness.

Peas going through a blast freezing tunnel.

Then came 'The Spanish Job' carried out by fieldsmen Jacklin and Warnes (see the supporting chapter).

In 1988, I had started a fledgling company, basically consisting of just myself and a YTS lad. It was called GRS Engraving, because that's what we did. By 1990, we had a staff of five and I was managing the company and growing our customer base, while at the same time still farming at Beacon Hill. In 1990, I had to regretfully hang up my Birds Eye hat.

It was several years before I got over the call of the pea harvest when I heard or saw viners in the vicinity, but only a well-steeped pea man will understand this feeling. Over the years I have been very happy to still be included in the Pea Gathering reunions of like-minded ex-Unilever fieldstaff, even though I was never a full-time employee.

The end product.

THE BIRDS EYE YEARS   63

Birds Eye staff Pat Jacklin, left, and Dave Warnes near Villafranca in Spain in May 1988.

CHAPTER EIGHT

The Spanish Job
May 1988

THE PHONE CALL
There was a phone call. I picked it up and the person on the other end of the phone said, "Hello, this is Colin, I have a little job for you, how are you fixed? Can you go to Spain for one or maybe two weeks in ten day's time?"

THE BRIEF
The brief was to go to Spain with my colleague Dave Warnes and get 1000t of peas at a decent tenderometer reading (TR) that had been frozen inside the two-and-a-half hour Birds Eye cut-off. We were to leave on Thursday 5 May from Heathrow, flying to Bilbao. Once there, we were to be picked up and taken somewhere in Spain by a driver from Alimentos Congelados SA (AC). The pay for the job was to be discussed another time, when Colin found out what it was.

JOURNEY TO HEATHROW
I drove down to Heathrow and had a most smooth and relaxing journey. Myself and Dave arrived at Walton-on-Thames and were met by Molly, the right-hand lady of Birds Eye's agricultural manager, John Bundy. She plied us with coffee and organised our taxi to the airport which turned out to be a Mercedes Executive runabout. That was the life.

THE PIONEER CORPS LEAVE BLIGHTY

We arrived at Heathrow in plenty of time. I had a bite to eat, but Dave was suffering from morning sickness at the thought of his forthcoming experience. Anyway, we had a run round of the duty free, during which Dave bought two films that would have been cheaper in Hammonds in Hull.

THE FLIGHT

Iberian Airlines can only be described as excellent. However, we were travelling in preferential class, my first experience of anything other than tourist class, and I was impressed.

THE ARRIVAL

We arrived at Bilbao about 9pm Spanish time. Fieldsman Dave Warnes and I were shepherded to one side and searched – our bags, cases, the lot. Finally, we got our undies back into our suitcases along with our wellies and wet gear. Dave did have a bit of trouble getting the air out of his blow-up doll, but eventually we were declared clean and fit for onward travel! We were met by Alphonso, the driver from AC, who drove us for two hours, leaving us at a place called Los Abetos, which was to be our home for the next three weeks.

Next morning, we surfaced about 8:00am to get coffee and a croissant for breakfast. At about 8:30am we were met by Julian Lizarazu, who had come to take us to the processing factory at Marcilla, where we talked about the job, the crops and the methods that were being used. This was followed by a guided tour of the factory. We also met and were introduced to members of the Alimentos Congelados (AC) staff, with whom we would be working.

Arrangements were made for us to pick up a Ford Orion car from Pamplona, some 35 miles away. Once again, our driver was Alphonso. He left us with our transport to get back to Marcilla, and what an experience it was driving in Pamplona.

THE FACTORY

The Alimentos Congelados factory at Marcilla was mixture of old and new, the latter consisting of some new and expensive equipment, such as an Elbiscan Sorter and a Cabin Plant Blancher. Size and brine grading are good additional assets for assuring a quality sample of peas, providing there is a market for the oversize peas and the brine floaters.

Dave Warnes, centre, with Casildo and Federico Alimentos Congelados (AC) fieldsmen near Fontella.

Hand vining peas into rice pudding tins to get a sample reading.

On inspection the factory seemed to have a very water costly process, with water everywhere and no apparent recirculation. Tipping peas directly from a lorry into an elevator was not ideal as it added another lorry into the shuttle system, in order to keep the peas fresh for Birds Eye use. The peas were weighed after cleaning and the growers were paid on the basis of this weight.

The factory only had one Tenderometer machine which was an FMC with a digital read out. This worked well but if the machine broke down, well, I suppose you had to guess the TR. We were told the factory capacity was around 9t an hour, however, the best output we saw them achieve was about 90t in 24 hours.

The final point of note was that although the factory left a bit to be desired, at best, the end product was comparable with home production.

THE FACTORY STAFF

Pedro was in charge and, after slimming down a bit, he weighed in at 145kg – a big lad! Pedro knew everything that went on, without exception, and he made all the production decisions at the factory.

Leonora was the wife of the late Placido, the boss of the company. She was very helpful and very ladylike, but well able to stand her ground if anyone ruffled her feathers.

Xavier was Alimentos Congelados' quality control man, a real cool cookie, with a dry sense of humour, but always helpful to Birds Eye staff.

Since the death of his late boss Placido, Julian was heading up the company with Leonora. Julian was a good man with a lot on his shoulders, but a genuine man you could discuss problems with.

THE FIELD STAFF

Julian and Pedro, whist not in the field themselves, oversaw the work of the fieldsmen.

Koldo was a good fieldsman with a great deal of knowledge, but he leant towards pressure from growers and had lost a few crops to political decisions.

Casildo probably had piles as he jumped around in his car while driving; his brother Pedro called him Emmerson Fitipaldi because of the way he drove. Casildo wore a different hat each day of the week, but no-one knew why! He was not your normal fieldsman, but having said that, he managed to bring his crops in on time.

Federico was a good fieldsman, totally on the ball with his judgement, who looked after the larger acreages in the south towards Gallur. However, on arrival at a pea field near Epila at 1:30pm we found Federico in a local bar having the fourth course of his lunch. I felt this kind of midday feasting by fieldsmen should be avoided in Hull.

Antonio was the jewel in the crown. He was about 5ft tall, wizened as a prune and bearing a strong resemblance to Sammy Davis Jnr. He had taken a lot of stick from his growers for low yields which they were associating with harvesting at a TR of 105. They were missing the point that the weather had been poor and the crops had suffered from some disease, which had reduced the yield. Antonio, as with Koldo, had many small fields, some as small as 1ha (2½ acres), so difficult to manage.

THE SAMPLING

Sampling was the only Spanish word that had a different meaning in English. You walked into a field and took a few vines out and when you had a slack handful you returned to your car, where you affixed a label, stating what part of Spain you were in, how many hectares you estimate there might be and any other pieces of information that may help you find the field again.

Dave, right, and Pedro at the Alimentos Congelados processing factory at Marcilla, Spain.

Tipping peas into the washer at Marcilla.

With the sample in your car boot, you rushed off to the factory, any time in the next 24 hours, when the sample would be hand podded into rice pudding tins (washed out) by girls from AC, or more likely by factory management with the help of Birds Eye field staff. The sample was then tested and hey presto, if it had a TR under 100, it was not ready to be vined, but if it was over 100, then it needed harvesting soon. We were told the crops were sampled three times a day, however, a lot was lost in translation as they actually meant three times in a season. Sampling left a bit to be desired!

MAPS, DRILLING LISTS & FIELD LOCATIONS

Apart from a map of the whole of Spain, maps of regions were not easy to come by, but we did find a map of Navarra and were able to copy a relevant portion showing villages and main roads, which was better than nothing. After two weeks in Spain we finally received a drilling list with the ink still wet. However, it was not complete and meant little to us. Field locations varied from on the side of main roads to places many miles from civilisation, off tracks with no markings. Even with a good memory, they could be very difficult to locate a second time.

THE FIELD SIZES

The fields varied in size from two acres up to 200 acres, not something we were used to seeing back in the UK. Within a 15km radius of the factory at Marcilla there were 80 fields of peas of around 1ha (2.5 acres). The field sizes were governed by two things. Firstly, was the area and the ownership of the land, which was often subject to an inheritance system.

In Navarra the field sizes were small, while in the south, at Aragon and Zaragoza, the fields were much bigger.

Secondly, another major factor in determining the field sizes were the irrigation systems that were being used. For example, in the south, large acreages were irrigated by large rotary booms with 40m sections joined together. In the north, irrigation was by means of small man-made channels and dykes with sluice gates, which could be opened to flood the land. It was primitive but effective, or so it seemed.

THE COUNTRY

Spain is a big country with many different facets. Most of us probably think of the holiday resorts of Malaga and Benidorm, but this is not the Spain of Navarra. The Ebro valley lies across the foothills of the Pyrenees. The river Ebro rises near Santander on the north coast and flows across to the Mediterranean at Tortosa, south of Tarragona. The Ebro is a major river like the Rhine or Trent, fed by river-sized tributaries like the Rio Aragon and Rio Arga, big rivers in their own right. These rivers are the reason for the region's fertility and irrigation opportunities, making it possible to grow a wide range of crops.

IN SPAIN, THE PEOPLE ARE RULED BY THREE MAIN BELIEFS

MANANA: This means what is not done today will be done tomorrow or the next day.

DOMINGO: This is Sunday, a day when everybody has a family day. It is not necessarily religious, but everyone enjoys this day. Perhaps apart from the pea season we could learn something from these people.

SIESTA: This is roughly the hours between 1pm and 4pm, when everything stops or at best slows down. All the men go to the bar (where there are no ladies), then they go home and this is when the Spanish babies are made!

Without these three pieces of culture, Spain could rule the world.

Four FMC pea viners working near Gallur in 1988.

CLIMATE

Although the climate we saw was by no means typical, we got a good cross section of the worst and best weather in this area. The temperature varied from 60F to 90F. On hot days the humidity was low, so it remained very comfortable.

There seemed to be a tendency to have three hot days followed by thunder storms which cleared the air and then the cycle repeated. We saw some very heavy rain fall, enough to stop the viners working. This was not a usual phenomenon as they generally expect a pleasant and warm climate at this time of the year.

THE CROPS

The peas we harvested were a mixture of good and bad, as we mostly see in England, probably due to heavy rain through much of the growing season. The drilling season had been very wet and we saw much uneven germination, however, there was no sign of foot rot, as we would expect to see in crops at home in wet conditions.

In some crops we saw very lush growth with poor pod fill and many signs of mildew and botrytis, resulting in poor yields from these crops. In some crops, mainly in the south, we saw good crops with good pod fill and yields up to 5t/ha. For the growers, this yield was very poor, as most years they expected up to 7-8t/ha.

OTHER CROPS

Also grown in the Navarra region were artichokes, asparagus, sweetcorn, peaches, spinach, grapes, tomatoes, apricots, potatoes, cauliflower, barley, wheat, oilseed rape. The specialities of the area were asparagus, cauliflower, sweetcorn and artichokes.

THE FIELD EQUIPMENT

The vining fleet consisted of 13 viners, namely two Ploegers and 11 FMC short drums. The Ploegers were on hire from somewhere in France. One machine was a year old, the other, which had been set up to start work in our peas, was new for the 1988 season.

The FMCs fell into three groups, with

FMC pea viners parked-up during a midday siesta near the town of Gallur in Spain.

four machines being 2-3 years old, a four further machines being 4-5 years old and the final three machines being over six years old. All the machines seemed to be reasonably maintained, however, the lack of safety guards left a bit to be desired.

One thing I did note was that when a viner came to a standstill with the drum stopped, four men would climb up on the walkway and open the covers. They then hung on to the nets while the driver dropped the machine into gear.

THE PEA TRANSPORT

The method of transporting the peas from the field to the factory consisted of trucks of mostly 20-25t, either eight or 10-wheelers, as opposed to the 10t types we were using back at home. On the other hand, any field within a 5-mile radius of the factory was likely to be serviced by farm tractors and trailers. On seeing this, John Linneker, one of the Birds Eye big cheeses, said, "How quaint, just like in California when I was there." The only concern I had was that they could have been leading pig manure beforehand and then on to peas, with very little hygiene being carried out on the trailer. I guess if it pleased top brass, I need not have worried!

Dave and myself organised shuttle services for the peas, ranging from one vehicle up to 13, bringing peas from as far away as 75-80 miles to meet the Birds Eye time specification.

THE ACCOMMODATION

We stayed at a hostel called Los Abetos, which lies between Cadrieta and Valtierra at a junction of the A15 and the NA134.

It was good by English or Spanish standards; the rooms were large and clean, but there was no TV.

Irrigation water channels like this one were common in the Navarra region of Spain.

Spanish service is slow, so you have to learn to calm down and go with the flow. The restaurant was good and there was a wide choice of food on the menu. Service at the table was excellent, with the food being served by local girls Beni, Pila and Beotri.

After two weeks we got the hang of the menu and despite our orders being placed in 'Spanglish', we got what we thought we had ordered 90% of the time.

Los Abetos, our Spanish home, during May 1988.

The view from my room at Los Abetos. This is where my underpants and socks took off in a gust of wind, from the window sill onto the flat roof. I had to give quick pursuit across the roof to gather up my underwear.

THE PROBLEMS

Radio contact between the factory and viners and then fieldsmen was perhaps satisfactory for Alimentos Congelados, but for a Birds Eye operation it was essential that Birds Eye field staff could contact the factory staff and vice versa, to give and receive updates on loads, timings, TRs and weights.

Language was a problem or at least a challenge, and even fieldsman Dave Warnes' crash course on Spanish code breaking could not solve this one. However, Spanglish, a delicate mix of 80% Spanish and 20% English, mostly won the day.

The Siesta, Domingo and Manana are unsurmountable problems still dominating Spanish Life.

Mosquitoes were a problem. The little critters could bite like alsatian dogs! My best count was 31 bites, many of which swelled up like golf balls. Dave had slightly less, but nearly caught one on his marriage tackle. I had warned him about over-exposure!

The driving in built-up areas in Spain is not for the faint-hearted, but even an Englishman can learn to drive like a Spaniard.

THE POTENTIAL

The area had great potential for many crops, with good soils in river valleys, irrigation and sunshine. The peas we harvested were of good quality, but it had been a difficult season and yields were not as high as they might have been in a normal year.

The most important thing I noticed was the willingness of Alimentos Congelados and especially Julian to give us just what we wanted. For example, in the drilling of crops as well as harvesting, he would be willing to be guided by Birds Eye. There was a

From left: Colin Wright, Pat Jacklin, Dave Warnes and Birds Eye's agricultural manager at that time, John Bundy, at the bar at Los Abetos.

real point to Julian's thought process. In 1992, Spain was joining the European Economic Community and they were in at the deep end. By 1992, Julian wanted to have his company ready to meet the demands of the wider market.

Getting peas harvested to Birds Eye standards was a new experience for the factory staff. Spain needed more than four years to get its act together agriculturally, but it got there in the end.

CONCLUSION

Dave and myself spent 22 days in fairly close contact, and during that time we were both pretty ill, probably after being eaten by mosquitoes. We did the job as we saw fit to get the required result, working mostly 12-hour days. At times I am sure we both had to bite our tongues so as not to cuss at each other. However, we did the job together. It would not have been easy to do it alone and certainly not as memorable. Spain is pretty wild in places, not to mention the wildlife and the people who call Navarra their home. Was it a success? With 1200t of good quality peas in the bag for Birds Eye, I guess it was.

CHAPTER NINE

Dave's retirement

This was my speech at the retirement party held for my friend and colleague, Dave Warnes.

So it has arrived at last, the long-awaited retirement of Bird's Eye fieldsman David Warnes, ex-RAF. I apologise for needing notes, but in order not to stray from the truth I thought it prudent to use a few prompts, rather than misalign an upstanding member of Unilever's field department.

When I was first posted to Hull in 1984 after the untimely demise of the Grimsby field department, I was introduced to David who was to be my mentor in looking after the fantastic Blue Group, which as you all know is the jewel in the crown of pea growing. David parted with the Blue Group like a surrogate mother who is breast feeding.

I must say Dave was a great help to me in those early days, when unknown growers and details of his favourite spots in the area were still a mystery to me.

Before we start on the Birds Eye story, Dave, let me pass on to you the good wishes of those now mature ladies that you knew so well when you were stationed in Her Majesty's Forces at North Somercotes in the Lincolnshire Marshes in the 1950s. They included Jean Moore, Julie Moss, Dorothy Wilkinson and Gwen Moore. to name but a few.

It came as a surprise to me that Dave was stationed in a concrete dug out near North Somercotes watching for the enemy to invade, because the last raiders we had down there had been the Vikings.

When I first arrived at the Hull factory on Hessle Road someone said to me: "David Warnes, he's a QC you know."

I said: "He seems alright to me."

What they meant was that he started his Birds Eye career in cryogenics in the quality department. I later realised this was why Dave had a pessimistic outlook on life and always set standards that no poor sod could achieve.

Dave told me some very important things when I relieved him of the Blue Group, as follows:

- Midges always appear on the 20 May at Monkton Walk. I spent three days looking for them and they came late in 1984.

- Poppies grow at Flower Hill Farm. I do not know why I remember that.

- Ron Clappison is a good chap.

- Colin does not like 'D' grade peas, they all need to be 'Sweet as a Nut'.

- Always underestimate the harvest yield; it protects your job.

- Bob bites! Bob was the black labrador at Cammidge and Robson's Flower Hill Farm that took a liking to Dave's nether regions. It was a sunny afternoon when radio silence was broken.

"Baker to Base, Baker to Base."

"Base to Baker, yes David, what can we do for you?"

"Simon, I've been savaged by a dog. I am looking in the wing mirror now, with my trousers down and he's drawn blood."

Such vivid memories of Dave and Birds Eye will always stay with me.

In 1988 Dave and myself were lucky enough to be asked to go to Spain to restock the pea larder. What an experience. Dave got homesick at Watford and remembered his aversion to flying when we got to Heathrow. We landed at Bilbao at about 10pm with a full complement of travellers on board. Going through customs D. Warnes and P. Jacklin were the only passengers to be stopped and singled out for Customs attention. Finally, we were allowed into Spain.

Once in Spain, Dave's gift of foreign languages really hit me. Had he been to night school to learn the language? I later found the Spanish were as mystified as I was.

On a more serious note, I would like to wish Dave a long and happy retirement, playing golf, choral singing, drinking and all the other things he will now have time for.

During a pea season I believe you see the best and worst of your colleagues and Dave's worst side was better than the rest of us.

All the best for the future, Dave.

Pat Jacklin, October 1997

The GRS Engraving & Sign Co. premises on No. 4 Westmour Units, Warwick Road, Fairfield Ind Estate, Louth.

CHAPTER TEN

The GRS Story 1988-2015

The story starts when my wife Judi and Martin Smith of GRS Electrical Engineers colluded to find me a job to fill in my spare time, now that we no longer had livestock on the farm in the winter months due to the changing patterns of farming.

A meeting was held with John Riggall, Martin Smith and Ian Gilliatt, the directors of GRS Electrical Engineers Ltd of 38, Northgate, Louth. The plan outlined by Martin Smith was that they had a hand pantograph engraving machine and a young person, Steve Tindall, still attached to ITEC on a Youth Training Scheme. They had a few orders coming in each month, netting about £100-£200 a month, with the most notable client being Yorkshire Electricity, which ordered a few labels each week. The plan was to see if I could find new customers and outlets for these engraved products. What I did not fully take on board was that I was going to run the job, while Steve did the engraving.

I agreed to go in to work for an hourly rate of pay. To begin the project I phoned and visited as many people as I could think of in the local area.

We had such a limited product to sell it made it difficult, but I did however find a few local people who wanted engraved labels and badges. It was nonetheless a modest, very low income beginning.

To start with I had a small desk in the same main office as the directors, but because both Ian Gilliatt and I had loud voices, it was suggested that I move into a side office with Malcolm Locking (I can take a hint!).

The engraving was done in a room over the archway into the property, probably no more than about 12ft x 12ft, but perfectly adequate for engraving purposes. As time went by it became clear that the people I talked to about sales required more than just labels. Local business contacts required safety signs and the ability for us to manufacture bespoke and corporate signs. I began to see potential, but also challenges ahead, maybe more equipment and at what cost? Perhaps more importantly, we had to have the ability to see designs through to manufacture, and keep in step with current legislation.

Along the way I was challenged with limited thinking and I thank John Riggall for his assistance in keeping a cool head in talking to Steve, who to be fair, was a young lad with no experience in either design or manufacturing. In 1989, John, myself and Steve went to London to look at computer-controlled engraving machines. We firstly assessed the Dahlgren machine at West Moseley, then went across to north-east London to see Gravograph and their VX 89 machine. We decided the Gravograph machine best suited our needs, and so we placed an order for I believe £8000-£9000.

GRS Engraving & Sign Co. staff Warwick Road, Louth, in 1993, from left: Pat Jacklin, Mandy Gilliatt, Joss Worthington, Tim Jacklin, Louise Arnold and Steve Tindall.

By 1990, my sales horizons had widened to cover Lincolnshire, Humberside and the East Midlands. Meeting the right people was essential, and so it was to this end that I booked stands at business exhibitions at Lincoln, Nottingham, Hull and Castle Donnington near East Midlands Airport. I held the belief that if potential serious buyers were kept waiting at one of these exhibitions, they might leave before I could get to see them, so I thought I needed to have a pleasant young lady to assist me, someone who could woo the punters until I could get to them for the hard sell (this is not me being sexist, it is a fact of life).

Louise Brooks helped at the first show at Lincoln, Judi at Nottingham (the most successful) and Pat Foxon at the Humber Bridge at Hull. The brief was 'keep them talking until I can get to them'. This system worked very well, but in hindsight it is alarming what promises I had to make about our capabilities!

Mandy and PHJ in 1993 at the time of GRS Engraving & Sign Co's BS5750 accreditation.

Pat Jacklin and Louise Brooks at an exhibition at Lincoln Showground in 1989.

The GRS Engraving & Sign Co. premises at the time of an extension to the building in 1996.

Following these exhibitions, telephone calls and personal visits, we began to build our client base. Our first serious order came from Paul McLintock at Conoco's procurement department. It was for about £800 of engraved labels and signs in spring 1988, so we were still in the pantograph era at this time. The staff in those early days consisted of Steve Tindall, Louise Brooks, Lee Shufflebotham and myself.

At this time I had an agreement with HiLite Signs to supply us on a daily basis with stock safety signs at a small discount off list price. Although they had many large companies that purchased from them, the difference was, if you ordered a sign from HiLite, you got delivery in a week. In contrast, if you bought it from GRS, Lee was on his bike after dinner to collect it and the signs would be dispatched via next day delivery. We bought Lee a T-shirt that said 'GRS Signs Roadrunner No Problem'.

In 1990, Louise left us to get married, and Judi and I went to her wedding at Wymondham in Norfolk. This left a gap in our plans for growth. When I told Judi she thought about it and through Jayne Turner, her work colleague, came up with her friend Mandy Benson, who had worked at Spencers newsagents and photography shop in Louth. Mandy thought she might be interested in the challenge (of working with me?), so in May 1990 she joined us.

We had by this time a small office/cupboard, about 10ft x 5ft, so when one person stood up the other had to sit down. Mandy did not engrave as her time was filled with dealing with customers, packing and dispatching orders, and perhaps most importantly tidying up my paperwork.

While we were in Northgate we did at least have access to a good supply of Cornish pasties from just around the corner in Vickers Lane

Following the exhibitions, we began to receive orders from British Steel and Ruston Gas Turbines at Lincoln, whose requirements were slowly increasing. In February 1991, we moved to Warwick Road on Fairfield Industrial Estate. At this time we were dedicated engravers, but also supplying some bought-in products as well, when requested.

It was at this time we got our first office computer, a Viglen Genie, which was subsequently stolen in a burglary.

THE GRS STORY 79

From this point on we were paddling our own canoe and in charge of our finances and wages, etc. During this early stage we started experimenting in the manufacture of Perspex and aluminium signs and looking at modular sign systems. It was a learning curve for all of us, especially me!

One thing that was not an unknown to me was how to talk to people and treat them, as this was something I had learnt whilst at Birds Eye. Thanks to my farming background, I was well-steeped in being frugal, which became a necessity as the company grew. From 1991 through to 2000, the growth was a steady upward curve, although I vividly remember the month of February 1991, just as we moved, being a low sales disaster, leaving me to ponder on our recent move and attempt at self-sufficiency.

During the following years we continued to add to our customer base, leading to a wide range of manufacturing requests, many of which were pioneering to us at the time. GRS became well-known in the field of signage for its quality and service. Between 1988 and 2015 we had a total of 70 staff pass through the books.

Employees are what make one company stand out from another, and it is with training and company policies in place that you can make that company outstanding. The company's eventual success was based on these two principles.

Without doubt, Mandy launched herself into the job to ensure we were successful. Her ability to sound knowledgeable in those early days, when she knew she was pushing her boundaries, was outstanding and left customers feeling content and satisfied. Her best skill was being honest with customers about delivery times and updating them if things changed.

Later, of course, she had as much skill as anyone, knowing the products fully and the methods of manufacture. My son Tim was a major factor in dealing

GRS Sign Co. vans at Warwick Road, circa early 2000s.

The staff of GRS Sign Co in March 2004, before the start of work on our new site in Tattershall Way on Fairfield Industrial Estate, Louth.

with customers on site, giving them assurances about products and their uses. As can be seen from the attached unsolicited testimonials, the GRS fitting teams were held in high regard by many of our prestigious clientele.

The rest of us just did our job in many supporting roles. From design, manufacturing, customer support and through to installation, it all seemed to work!

As the 1990s progressed our client list got longer and the companies more prestigious. It was at this time we embarked on achieving BS 5750, or as it was later called ISO 9000. Although several of our clients requested we conform to this standard in order to continue selling products to them, that was not the main reason we sought this level of accreditation. We believed that such a system would work and give us a sound set of procedures to work to, and this proved to be the case.

The back of GRS Sign Co's original Warwick Road building, with the new site in foreground.

THE GRS STORY   81

A sample of the engraved labels produced by GRS Sign Co. for Conoco, Siemens, British Steel and many more.

It was in 1993 that Ian Gilliatt approached me and asked if I would like to buy his shares in the partnership, so in his words, "I could have a slice of the action." This was my entry into the partnership with John and Martin, who were almost sleeping partners, leaving me to run the company as I saw fit.

Our sales strategy was to enlist companies who made timely requests on their orders and would pay on time without monthly chasing. This system was successful and only a few potential clients were turned away because they did not meet this criteria.

In 1995, following a sales meeting with Mandy, Judi, Tim and Steve, we decided to target the health and education sectors as prospective purchasers, as all political parties are keen to be seen to be supporting both of these areas.

In 1990, whilst still at Northgate, Martin Smith had an appointment with Peter Metcalf of Crownship Developments that he had been unable to keep, so he asked me to stand in and assess if we could make use of his services.

Peter arrived and told me about his company's portfolio and the training programmes they were running. After a few days Peter contacted me again and we discussed how our small company could benefit. We decided it was me who needed the first injection of training, so I signed up for a Business Development Course at The Petwood Hotel, Woodhall Spa, on a monthly basis after work.

Together with five other people from small companies, we became The Petwood Group. The strength was in Peter's leadership and the group's ability to set each other business challenges, which would be answered at the next monthly meeting. This was a great incentive to get things done, I suppose down to peer pressure as much as anything. I well remember having a difficult member of staff and the group's response was, "If you've got a lemon, it will never be an orange, get rid of it." In a small business you sometimes need someone to sound ideas off, and this was that place.

Over time and for the next 25 years, Peter ran courses for me and my GRS staff on many topical issues, such as communication, body language, team building and many more. Peter is still a good friend and I thank him for his input and support to my whole team over the years.

From the mid-1990s we got fully into manufacturing bespoke signage for our clients. Engraving continued to be a big part of our output, but with the addition of vinyl cutters and later full colour printers in-house, it gave us ever wider opportunities to find new markets.

It was in the late 1990s that a bombshell dropped, when the original company, GRS Electrical Engineers Ltd, ran into financial difficulties not of its own making.

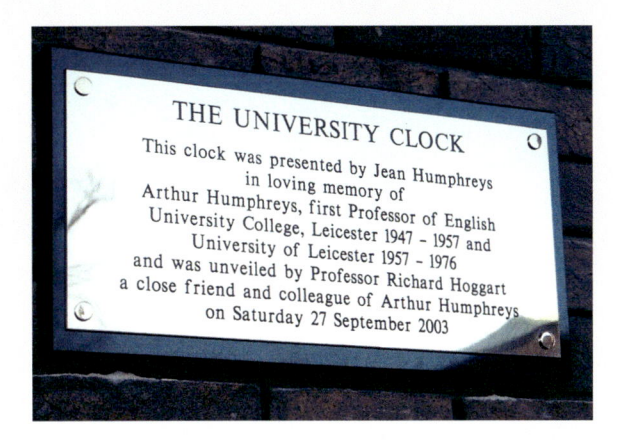

This brass plaque was made by GRS Sign Co. for the University of Leicester.

One of the corporate types of modular signage used by the University of Leicester, a customer of GRS Sign Co.

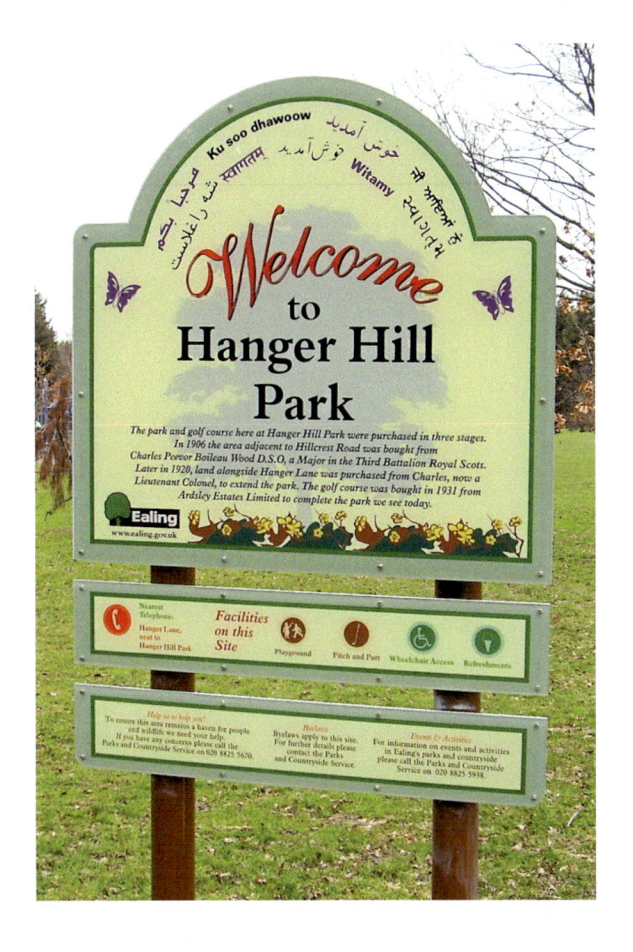

Huddersfield University commissioned GRS Sign Co. to produce this stainless steel plaque to mark the opening of a refurbished building at its facility.

One of the many park and amenity site signs produced by GRS Sign Co. for the London Borough of Ealing.

Signage for a new sports facility that was built by the University of Wolverhampton.

THE GRS STORY 83

THE EQUIPMENT USED BY GRS SIGN COMPANY

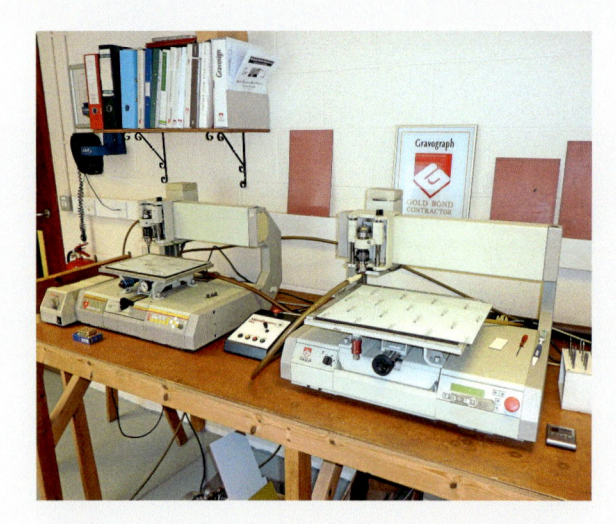

Two more Gravograph engravers; one is a VX 89 model, the other an IS 600.

The Gravograph IS 800 computerised engraver used by GRS Sign Co.

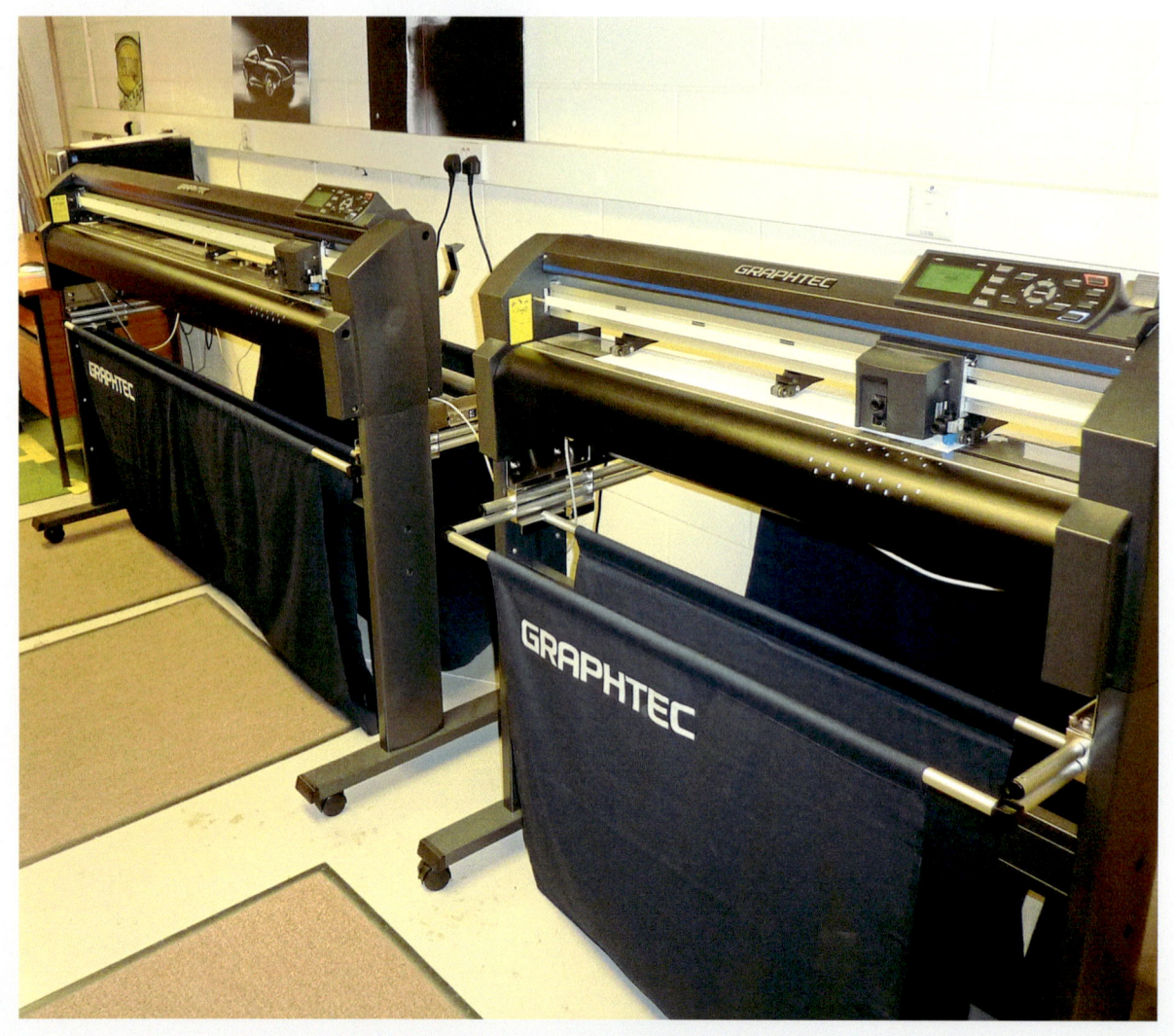

Two Graphtec vinyl cutting machines.

84   **C. R. JACKLIN & SON AT BEACON HILL FARM**

One of the Mimaki CJV 130 full colour printers that was used by GRS Sign Co.

Part of the racking and storage area for parts used in the manufacturing process.

A Gravograph LS 100 laser engraver.

THE GRS STORY 85

Start of the new GRS Sign Co. building on Tattershall Way, Fairfield Industrial Estate, Louth, in April 2004.

This left our company very vulnerable and so after taking advice, I made an offer to my two partners to buy their shares in the partnership and sever ties with their company.

Our strategy on health and education began to pay off, as the Royal Hospital Chesterfield and Pilgrim Hospital at Boston became our first hospital signage customers. Other hospitals that followed to become regular customers were Louth County, Diana Princess of Wales at Grimsby, Scunthorpe General, Goole, Lincoln County, Grantham, Leicester University Hospitals (The General, The Royal and Glenfield), Sheffield Teaching Hospitals (The Hallamshire and Northern General) and Hull Royal Infirmary and Castle Hill. As well as hospitals we also gained many Primary Care Trusts and GP practices. This was a successful strategy that we continued to follow until 2015.

It was a similar story with educational facilities. Our first major achievement here was with the University of Leicester, which Mandy and I had visited, to find that they had a signage tender that was about to close. We did our best to charm the procurement manager, who gave us the opportunity to quote if we could do it quickly.

We were successful and became the university's signage supplier up to 2015. Leicester, at that time, was a top ten English university, so it was good for our credibility that we were able to service such contracts. Leicester was followed by Wolverhampton, Huddersfield, Salford, Leeds Metropolitan and Lincoln, where we held term contracts for signage. With the exception of Leeds Metropolitan and Lincoln, the rest were still going strong up to our close in October 2015.

In addition to hospitals we also worked for colleges, secondary and primary schools, as well as nurseries.

However, this was only part of our story as we had many regular 'blue chip' companies as customers, including British Steel at Scunthorpe and Redcar, Conoco Gas Terminal at Theddlethorpe and Humber Refinery, Du Pont at Wilton Teeside, Ruston Gas Turbines (later Siemens) at Lincoln, The London Borough of Ealing, East Lindsey Distict Council, the list goes on.

One day after Judi had retired from her job at Bridge McFarland she came in and was looking round the workshop at the signs being manufactured. She said, "How do you do it?" The simple answer, other than it being down to training and trust, was "I do not know."

Mandy's role had become ever-more pivotal in terms of customer contact and steering much of the production team. She used to say, "I am not here to be popular," and she was right, not that in any way she ever did things to make life difficult for the staff. But she told them the truth and what was required of them to achieve customer satisfaction.

In 2003 it became clear that our premises at 2 and 4 Westmour Units, Warwick Road, were becoming inadequate to turn around the major jobs we were securing. A directors meeting was held with Judi, Mandy, Tim, Steve and myself, at which I proposed a move to a new building. After raising a few eyebrows, everyone agreed, so we negotiated to buy a plot of land directly behind our existing building, looking onto Tattershall Way, from East Lindsey District Council at a cost of £70,000.

The next challenge was the construction of a purpose-built property. We did have some ideas about this as we had looked round other sign companies and in our opinion saw bad practices caused by poorly laid-out workspaces.

This was something we could improve on in the layout of our new building. Jim Fairburn constructed the building and Gary Cooper was our clerk of works. The build started in April 2004 and was completed for us to move into in September 2004.

The new building on Tattershall Way starting to take shape in May 2004.

GRS Sign Co. Ltd's new building on Tattershall Way in August 2006. The three vans were used by the company for signage contract service work.

The new build was known as the Beacon Project. The question of how to finance it was foremost in my mind during the planning process, what with the total cost of the land, new build and all associated costs being some £400,000. To cover this expense we had two properties to sell, plus we received a small grant from EMDA, leaving us with a mortgage to cover the balance of £167,000 over the next 15 years.

At this point I should say what good relationships I had always had with my accountant Steve Czornyj and bank managers David Mapletoft and Paul Gray at Barclays and later Adrian Stapley at Yorkshire Bank. I saw them as a company asset and not a necessary evil, and as such I always kept them in the loop with both good and bad news. As for Steve Czornyj, every move I made that involved finance or any risk to the company, was always shared with him before any actions were taken. Looking back this was a huge challenge for such a small company, but it was essential for us to maintain the service to our customers.

The main entrance sign at Conoco's Humber Refinery was manufactured by GRS Sign Co.

By 2004 we were competing against

88   C. R. JACKLIN & SON AT BEACON HILL FARM

national sign companies for work and were taking a good market share. The site visits by Mandy and myself always resulted in more jobs either to supply or supply and fit. The sales office became a hub alive with sales enquiries and preparing job sheets for the manufacturing side.

Manufacturing now consisted of four computerised machine engravers, one Laser engraver, two Grahtec vinyl cutters and two wide print Mimaki printers. Staffing peaked at 16 staff which included two installation teams, and most of the time things were buzzing.

In late 2008 and early 2009 we noticed a downturn in our monthly sales, which turned out to be the start of the banking crash, reported by official sources some six months later. As 2009 progressed it became clear there was a significant drop in sales numbers and also in sales values.

We decided to hold a meeting with all staff to fill them in on the situation. At the meeting I outlined the current situation regarding sales and what action we might need to take in the form of reduced working hours and other cost-saving options.

The inspiration for this foundation stone at GRS Sign Co's new premises came from the stones that had been set into buildings at Beacon Hill Farm over the years.

I put a plan forward to reduce the working hours from 40 down to 38 and working until midday on a Friday, effectively giving a 4½ day working week. These plans were to enable the company to keep all its staff in employment. Reluctantly, the staff agreed in order to protect everyone's income.

The south-west elevation of GRS Sign Co Ltd's premises on Tattershall Way on Fairfield Industrial Estate, Louth.

GRS Sign Co's managing director Pat Jacklin at his desk in the sales office of the company's premises on Tattershall Way.

It was at this time the bank requested an audience to tell us they needed to reduce their book liability, although we need to remember it was the banks who had caused the problem and were now struggling themselves. We had a bank overdraft facility for £30,000, which we had not used for a number of years, but I believed it was good business practice to have it in place.

Like my staff, I reluctantly agreed to cancel the facility and pay off the small amount still owing on our building mortgage. From this point on I was the sole financial backer for GRS Sign Co – personally!

All our regular customers continued to place orders but for lower values. It was a difficult period, but we tightened our belt and got on with the new normal. I can say that from 2009 to 2015, a period of 84 months, we had only one month that showed a trading loss. So we managed to stay financially healthy, but for the time being the days of sales growth had gone. This was a worrying time, especially when you have staff relying on you and you only have your own resources to back the company up, if it should require it.

In 2012 I had reached the age of 68 and was starting to think about winding down from running the company every day. Mandy and Tim were both looking to their futures in their own directions, and so with myself and my two main people not going to be there in the longer term to run the company, I decided to

Pat Jacklin's desk in the main sales office. The office was located in the northern end of GRS Sign Co's premises, on the first floor.

90   C. R. JACKLIN & SON AT BEACON HILL FARM

discuss with Steve Czornyj a course of action to sell the company as a going concern, protecting jobs.

For the next two years we had various options ongoing and some personal contacts who we weighed up to see if they could fit the bill. Sadly, all these efforts yielded no positive result for the long-term security of the company and its staff. At a directors' meeting in June 2015, I put forward a proposition to the directors to scrap all that had gone before and sell the property and all the sign-making equipment and other assets and pay the staff redundancy. Discussion took places and it seemed like a plan that might work.

On the 22 June 2015 we engaged Phil Stevens as agent, and on 23 June 2015 he had a prospective local buyer. On 24 June 2015 the buyer accepted the contract at the asking price, for the land and building.

The next job was to begin marketing our sign-making equipment. We received an offer for our laminator which we accepted, but this and the Vauxhall Astra van were the only two bits of kit we sold, as out of the blue we had interest from a company in Lincoln who eventually went on to purchase the company, less premises, which we had already sold.

After lengthy discussions the deal was done and a compromise settlement was arrived at.

GRS Sign Co Ltd ceased to trade on Friday 30 October 2015. I was then a free man, ready for the next challenge.

Meetings with customers and suppliers took place around this desk in the sales office on the first floor of GRS Sign Co's Tattershall Way premises. This is also where company managing director Pat Jacklin and office manager Mandy Gilliatt carried out all the major pricing of jobs and contracts.

BARCLAYS

Sort Code:
20-50-21

BARCLAYS BANK PLC
CORPORATE BUSINESS CENTRE
P.O. Box No. 294, City Office Park, Tritton Road, Lincoln LN6 7YY

24th November 1999

Mr P H Jacklin
GRS Engraving & Sign Company
4 Westmour Units
Warwick Road
Fairfield Industrial Estate
Louth   LINCS   LN11 0YB

Our Ref. PSG/JSC

Dear Pat

It was useful for us to meet again recently, continuing our existing close working relationship built over the past 4 years as a customer of the Corporate Banking Team here in Lincoln.

Clearly, throughout our 12 year banking relationship, it is evident how highly you prioritise the awareness of the financial needs of your business. We do value your regular contact, particularly prior to taking on board substantive additional work with regard to the impact on funding, cashflow or dealing with any potential problems that may arise.

I wish you well with the present tender you are making for the sign writing work in respect of Yorkshire Water, which I believe falls well within the capability of your business to comfortably fulfil and, subject to the repayment terms being met, this additional work will sit comfortably within with present work portfolio.

I look forward to following your progress.

Yours sincerely

P S Gray
Corporate Manager

Direct Line: (01522) 343514

Regulated by IMRO and the Personal Investment Authority.
Barclays Bank PLC represents only the Barclays Marketing Group for life assurance, pensions and unit trust business.
Registered in London, England. Reg. No: 1026167. Reg. Office: 54 Lombard Street, London EC3P 3AH

1595 (6/99)

Letters of recommendation from Barclays, Pilgrim Hospital and David S. Smith for GRS Sign Co.

your ref:

our ref:

date: 6 December 1999

TO WHOM IT MAY CONCERN

Pilgrim Hospital

Sibsey Road, Boston
Lincolnshire PE21 9QS
Tel: 01205 364801
Fax: 01205 354395
Minicom (for the deaf):
01205 365685

GRS Engraving and Sign Company

GRS Engraving and Sign Company have been known to me for some 10 years. Over this time in my capacity as Capital Projects Manager I have found them to be efficient, economical and reliable. Their fixing service is of the same high standard culminating into an exemplary sign company. It has always been the practise of my Trust to award business based upon competition, but in the case of signage I have been confident GRS are competitive and in most cases not sought competition. In the few exceptions where competition has been exercised, GRS have won our business with good margins proving their ethos of excellent service with economy.

They are a medium sized signage company with a friendly service capable of tackling a 'one off' or a major scheme of up to £20,000 in value. Hospital signage is a specialisation and perhaps their forte, but I am aware they also specialise in corporate identity signage as well as providing signage advice.

There are many signage companies in today's market place each promising the same excellent service with economy. Sadly very few can deliver these promises and fail miserably. If you cannot accept failure and require a job done right first time, I recommend you speak to GRS.

Alternatively, you may wish to speak to the many other satisfied customers. I can only be one of many.

Signed as a true and totally unsolicited statement

L C Hartley
Capital Projects Manager

Chairman P J Jordan   Chief Executive J J Somers   Pilgrim Health NHS Trust

David S Smith Corrugated
PACKAGING

Fordham Road
Newmarket
CB8 7TX
Tel: 01638 722100
Fax: 01638 722101 (General)
Fax: 01638 722102 (Sales)

CU/jhb

09 December 1999

TO WHOM IT MAY CONCERN

During late 1996 and early 1997, David S Smith Packaging built a new state of the art purpose built factory on a greenfield site near Cambridge.

Like may companies, to begin with, we under-estimated the amount of input needed to successfully sign a new site. WE had many discussions with the Building Inspector and Fire Officers who did little to give definitive answers to our questions. Through this period of time GRS Sign company sat in on meetings advising action on signage throughout. Their prior knowledge of such sites was a great help to myself, who had by now been put totally in charge of signage to get the new factory ready for production and the opening by HRH Prince Philip, Duke of Edinburgh.

The GRS Sign Company designed, manufactured and fitted all signage on this mult-million pound prestigious site.

I would have no hesitation in trusting this company with other large jobs for my company. The advice and support of GRS, which was an uncharged item, certainly made the cost of signage good value for money.

pp. *[signature]* MD.

Colin Usher
Divisional Technical Projects Manager

C:\All Files\Word\Sales\David Coleman\GRS signage reference 9 Dec 99.doc   Sonia Davies
David S Smith Corrugated is a division of David S Smith Packaging Limited.
Registered in England No. 501594
Registered Office: 4-16 Artillery Row, London SW1P 1RZ.

Certificate N°. FM 12254

CHAPTER ELEVEN

About the Author

(optional reading)

From a speech made by the author, Pat Jacklin,
on his 70th birthday in March 2014

I thought I would write a timeline of some of the events that have shaped my life. Upon reading through, it occurred to me that it reads a bit like a eulogy, so I will keep it handy for a later event!

I was born at 9pm on Sunday 19 March 1944 in the front room at Beacon Hill Farm, Grainthorpe. In April 1949 I started School at Marshchapel County Primary School, and on 10 September 1951 I went to St. James Choir School in Grimsby. I left in 1960 after being the head boy during my final year, an honour I look back on with some pride and affection.

In 1954, while aged 10, I became a member of the 1st North Somercotes Boy Scouts. Again, I look back on this time and realise how much I learnt from my Scouting days. Highlights included the World Scout Jamboree I attended at Sutton Coldfield in 1957, and the two weeks I spent in Belgium, Luxembourg and Holland in 1958. Taking a group of scouts to Great Tower Scout Camp on the side of Windermere was another highlight. We took another group to a camp at Ventnor on the Isle of Wight, and spent many weekends at camps at Donna Nook.

After leaving school I joined the Old Boys Association and played rugby for that team in a Lincolnshire league, as well as playing for the Grimsby Colts. After leaving school I attended Grimsby College to complete the A level in Biology that I had started while still at St. James Choir School.

From 1959 through to 1962 I undertook City & Guilds courses on Crop Husbandry, Animal Husbandry, Agricultural Machinery and Farm Records and Accounts. These courses were held in Louth and Grimsby over a four-year period, with additional residential teaching taking place at Riseholme Agricultural College, near Lincoln.

After leaving school I started working on the farm for my Dad, earning £4. 10s. 0 a week, plus board and lodge. Mostly this went well, but as with many father and son working arrangements, inevitable differences can emerge. Although we did not always agree, my Dad was never against new ideas if they seemed reasonable and affordable. We undertook to take part in the Small Farm (Business Management) Scheme, which required us to plan three years in advance and state how we would increase production, with records being kept to validate the achievement. In return, we would get about £100 per year for being part of the scheme, but only if we succeeded in achieving what we had aimed for.

In 1965, we purchased a new

International B-414 tractor. I say 'we' because I was lucky to be included in the partnership C. R. Jacklin & Son that was set up by my mother and father. At this point in the mid-1960s I believe we began to progress to using a few modern farming practices, at least as much as the farm finances would allow.

To help support me being on the farm, my Dad always made himself available to assist neighbours with threshing and other jobs to bring in a bit of extra income, leaving me to do the yard work and feeding the pigs, calves and cattle.

So that's how the 1960s looked at Beacon Hill Farm.

In 1967, when I married Jennifer, the financial strain of two families living off such a small acreage really began to show. From this point on it was me who went out to do the extra jobs to boost the farm income.

In 1970, we took our first package holiday with Clarksons at a cost of £35 for 10 days in Benidorm, flying there and back with Court Airlines in a BAC 111.

The month of May 1971 saw the arrival of our first child, Timothy Edward, who was followed in October 1972 by our daughter, Nina Louise.

Over the years I have played squash at Louth Golf Club, and sailed my Minisail dinghy at Covenham Reservoir, Ruislip, Doncaster, Swanage Bay, Ullswater and many other places. In my late teenage years I covered many miles with my Le Brun bike, of which I was very proud. I was a bell ringer, using both handbells and church bells, and the high spot of my campanology was ringing a peal of Grandsire Doubles (1250 changes).

Through my younger years, although an only child, I was lucky to have great family support from both my mother's family and my father's side. I always got cards from uncles and aunts on birthdays and regular visits meant the family was always in touch. For many reasons, these practices do not seem quite the same these days.

In the 1970s I drove pea cutters for Roy Scaman and Don Brader, working 12-hour shifts during the months of June and July. I also helped Tony Hastings to repair and maintain the four Mather & Platt pea viners operated by the Binbrook Pea Growers group.

Tony and myself also built several corn silos, starting with two at Beacon Hill Farm and others for G. Lowis, North Somercotes, the Crust family at Burgh on Bain and Washingborough near Lincoln, and grain conveyors and elevator systems at Dawsons' Tin Town Farm at North Somercotes. It was whilst doing this installation, up in the roof, that both Tony and I realised we did not much like working at heights. Just after this Tony bought Fotherby Lawnmowers and again I helped him with garden machinery repairs and servicing.

In 1974, I joined the Louth Lions Club, of which I became President twice, Secretary twice, Zone Chairman and also Region Chairman. I was an active member of the club for 29 years and thoroughly enjoyed the camaraderie. I still fully believe in the objects and ethics of Lionism. My wife Judi and I have made many friendships through our involvement with the Lions, including Derek and Aileen, Tony and Rita and Steve and Helen, plus countless others over the years, including our good friends in Bad Konigshofen in Northern Bavaria in Germany.

In 1977 I was invited to Birds Eye at Grimsby to look at running the Field Operations for the agricultural department, from 6pm through to 6am, for the duration of the pea harvest. I did this job for seven years at Grimsby until the pea operation closed at Ladysmith Road and moved to Hessle Road in Hull. I do not think I was the reason they closed the Grimsby site! Whilst at Hull I looked after two pea harvesting groups. The one on the Yorkshire Wolds covered from Market Weighton in the west to Beverley in the east. My other group was growing peas from Caenby Corner in the south to South Ferriby on the bank of the River Humber.

My last proper job with Birds Eye was in 1988, when I was asked to go to Spain to assist with overseeing the harvesting of 1000 tons of peas to Birds Eye standards. A 10% free offer had cleaned the stocks out in the UK and consequently we needed to get new crop peas back in the freezer, a month before the English crop was ready.

What an experience it was spending five weeks living and working in the Ebro Valley, south of Pamplona, speaking 'Spanglish', mainly to order food, and dealing with the mosquito bites and later malaria-like symptoms that lasted for 2-3 years.

In 1987, my wife Judi had a chance conversion with Martin Smith of GRS Electrical, when he came in to look at a job for her employer, the local firm of solicitors, Bridge McFarland. Judi was working full-time as an Office Manager and Accounts Clerk for the company.

Because of changing farming patterns (by now we had no cattle to look after through the winter months), she found that when she got home, exhausted after a long day's work,

that I was full of life and raring to go. So Judi asked Martin if he had a job for me.

GRS is another story, however, it is in good health and still going strong, with 15 staff and some excellent customers, built up over 26 years by Mandy and the team.

In 2002, I asked Judi what she would like to do, apart from shopping (I am allergic to it!). She said she would like to go bowling. We had been members of Louth Indoor Bowling Club (LIBC) since 1995, so reluctantly I took her. At this time Judi's eyesight was failing, but she found she could adapt to bowling by using a monocular, and duly went on to become a successful bowler at club and county level.

Bowling, like the stories of GRS and C. R. Jacklin & Son, would need a full evening, so it will have to be told another day. Today, I am vice-President of Louth Indoor Bowling Club and I bowl at Louth Bowling Club, situated across from St. Marys Churchyard in the town. Louth Bowling Club was founded in 1908 and has a full and documented history. The first President of the club was Canon Albert Wilde who in 1909 married my Grandad and Grandma Jacklin at St. James Church.

Nowadays, I treat farming as relaxation and enjoyment, unlike the 1960s and 70s when we relied on the farm for our main living.

Looking back, if we can say we left things better than we found them, then I guess the mission was successful.

CHAPTER TWELVE

Future prospects

For the past 83 years, determination and pride, together with hard work, have been the driving forces that have kept Beacon Hill Farm a business, a home and a place for us to be proud of. We have a legacy dating back to 1938 and perhaps even earlier to 1911 to protect and respect.

As we approach 2022, we have a whole list of challenges facing the business that were unheard of in previous years, these being as follows:

- Aftermath of Brexit.
- Covid 19.
- Introduction of more environmentally friendly farming policies.
- Using the land as a buffer against climate change, and climate change itself.
- Rising sea levels in this marshland area of Lincolnshire.
- Volatile markets for grain, fertiliser, fuel, etc.

On the negative side is the size of the farm, currently 82 acres, which offers no benefits in terms of purchasing power and striking deals for contracting services.

On the upside, the land is in good heart and has not been abused with cropping options, heavy machinery and untimely cultivations in bad conditions. The equipment used is of a good modern standard and the contractors that we currently use are doing a good job for us using high-spec equipment.

GOING FORWARD
We have entered a Mid-Tier environmental land management agreement, which we can transfer to a new environmental scheme when the powers that be decide on their requirements. This will help to counter the loss of the Basic Payment Scheme to some small extent.

Of course, what we as farmers really need is sales and purchases to be in sync with one another over a period of years, to enable cropping plans to be put in place that will provide food for human consumption and animal rations for the domestic market, while also allowing us to export the surplus to help the country's balance of payments.

In the meantime, the quality of life that the farm provides us with will continue to give us satisfaction, providing we continue to do things in a timely fashion, grow the right crops to suit the prevailing market requirements, and use tried and tested procedures to carry out our agricultural activities.

We must be prepared to offer the farm the financial backing it needs through the challenging periods that will occur. If we expect the farm to cover its own costs, but expect no personal financial benefit, then we will not be disappointed, although we may be pleasantly surprised from time to time.

The person responsible for the farm will have to continue to earn his main living elsewhere, but the farm and its land are still a huge asset for future generations and will continue to give

Three generation of Jacklins.
From left: Tim, Harry, and Pat Jacklin in February 2022.

great enjoyment and satisfaction from seeing a job well done, even allowing for the extreme pressure of 21st century trends that have seen farming enterprises becoming ever-larger.

It is further encouraging that my grandson, Harry, the fourth generation of the Jacklin family to live at Beacon Hill Farm, is looking to take his tractor driving test after his 16th birthday in January 2022. Good Luck Harry.

God Speed The Plough.

POSTSCRIPT

Short Update

As we enter 2022, a short update on life at Beacon Hill Farm is perhaps in order.

Our new tractor, a Case IH Luxxum 120, ordered in June 2021 and due for delivery in October 2021, finally arrived in the yard of supplying dealer, Louth Tractors, in February 2022.

Our Explorer barley, sold for November 2021 movement, is still in store and we've been told that it will be moved at the end of January 2022. A final part-load of wheat is also due to exit our ownership, but I do not know when yet.

We had a good harvest in 2021, with only the wheat, which had certainly looked capable of producing 4t/acre, being slightly disappointing at 3.2t/acre due to low bushel weights. Happily, the higher commodity prices have more than compensated for the lower yield.

We got the whole farm drilled during the autumn of 2021. Our 30 acres of Tundra winter beans and 50 acres of Skyscraper winter wheat are all looking good at the time of writing this Postscript (January 2022).

However, as the wheat emerged it became obvious to the world that I had inadvertently left a few skylark plots when I drilled the field! So, on reflection, after 60 years as the drillman at Beacon Hill Farm, I have decided to pass the job over to Tim, who I am sure will do a good job.

Most of the land, some 64 acres, was min-tilled prior to being drilled, with the remaining 17 acres being ploughed. I keep consulting my Freams Elements of Agriculture book to see if there is a true long-term benefit to min-till crop establishment on heavy marshland soil? Perhaps it is to save the planet and store carbon, in order that the masses can still jet off around the world in aircraft to evermore endangered environments! I have not yet found the exact page in Freams that gives me the answer to my questions, but I am still hopeful.

I have discussed the subject with Tim, my son and farming partner, and we are willing to give the environment a chance with our 80 acres, but at the same time we do still wish to be part of the food chain that feeds an ever-growing worldwide population.

Pat Jacklin, January 2022

C. R. Jacklin & Son's new Case IH Luxxum 120 in Louth Tractors' yard on 15 February 2022.

FIELD VIEWS - 2019-2022

Ploughing marshland soil.

Winter wheat, two months after drilling.

Vining peas at Beacon Hill in 2019.

Field margin down Ings Lane.

Explorer spring barley.

Planet spring barley.

LESSONS LEARNT

Be true to your own principles.

Listen to advice and then judge for yourself.

Treat others as you would wish to be treated.

Get used to paddling your own canoe.

*Personal relationships in business
and in life are essential.*

*Always look at the big picture
and not the close up snap.*

*Communication is an essential skill;
the sooner it is, learnt the better.*

Always pay your way and do not expect favours.

*Satisfaction in what you do is essential
for a happy and content existence.*

*Always make decisions for the right reasons,
not just the convenient ones.*

The author, Pat Jacklin, and his wife Judi.

◆ ACKNOWLEDGEMENTS ◆

*I am indebted to my late mother and father for being custodians
of so much history, which has allowed me to pick up the pieces
and keep the story alive into its second century.*

*I am grateful to my wife, Judi, for her support while writing the book and
later her constructive criticism to help make the reading more presentable.*

*Thank you to Rory Day, editor of Classic Tractor magazine, and designer Craig Lamb
of Kriele Limited of Horncastle for presenting and publishing the book as I requested.*

*Thank you to my former Birds Eye colleague David Warnes,
whose own book 'Beverley before I forget' provided the inspiration
for the title of the 'Wragholme before I forget' chapter in this book.*

*Finally, thanks to Freddie Bushby and Andrew Greenwood for the use of
the photographs they allowed me to use in the illustration of this book.*